DESKTOP PUBLISHING ASSIGNMENTS

J Alan Lyon
Head of Section
Donald C Maclean
Senior Lecturer

Office Administration and Technology Section
Dundee College of Further Education

HEINEMANN EDUCATIONAL

Heinemann Educational Publishers
Halley Court, Jordan Hill, Oxford OX2 8EJ
a division of Reed Educational & Professional Publishers Ltd

MELBOURNE   AUCKLAND   FLORENCE
PRAGUE   MADRID   ATHENS   SINGAPORE
TOKYO   SAO PAULO   CHICAGO   PORTSMOUTH (NH)
MEXICO   IBADAN   GABORONE   JOHANNESBURG
KAMPALA   NAIROBI

© J Alan Lyon and Donald Maclean

First Published 1993
96 11 10 9 8 7 6 5 4 3

A catalogue record for this book is available from the British Library on request

ISBN 0 435 45141 3

Printed in Great Britain by Bath Press Ltd Bath

All rights reserved. No part of this publication may be reproduced, stored in a retrieval system, or transmitted, in any form, or by any means, electronic, mechanical, photocopying, recording, or otherwise, without the prior written permission of the publishers.

This book is sold subject to the condition that it shall not, by way of trade or otherwise, be lent, resold, hired or otherwise circulated, in any form of binding or cover other than that in which it is published, without the publisher's prior consent.

CONTENTS AND INDEX

Section		Page
1	Preparation of Publications (Assignments 1-12)	5
2.1	2-column Publications (Assignments 13-16)	17
2.2	2-column Publications with vertical ruling (Assignments 17-20)	21
2.3	2-column Publications with vertical ruling and framing (Assignments 21-24)	25
2.4	2-column Publications with vertical ruling, framing and header (Assignments 25-28)	29
3	Publications with framing for subsequent import of illustrations (Assignments 29-32)	33
4.1	3-column Publications (Assignments 33-36)	37
4.2	3-column Publications with header (Assignments 37-40)	41
4.3	3-column Publications with header and footer (Assignments 41-48)	45
4.4	3-column Publications with header, footer and framing (Assignments 49-52)	53
5.1	2-page Publications (Assignments 53-56)	57
5.2	2-page Publications (2 columns portrait) (Assignments 57-60)	65
5.3	2-page Publications (3 columns landscape) (Assignments 61-64)	73
5.4	2-page Publications (4 columns landscape) (Assignments 65-68)	81
6	4-page Publications (2 columns) (Assignments 69-72)	89
7	2-page Publications (5 columns landscape) (Assignments 73-76)	105
8	Scanning illustrations and fitting (Assignments 77-80)	113
9	Scanning illustrations and custom wrap (Assignments 81-84)	117
10	2-up, 3-up, 4-up, 8-up, 10-up, 12-up Publications (Assignments 85-94)	121
11	Design of forms (Assignments 95-98)	131
12.1	Scanning illustrations and placing (Assignments 99-102)	135
12.2	Illustrations for scanning (Assignments 103-114)	139

DESKTOP PUBLISHING ASSIGNMENTS

ABOUT THIS TEXT

The authors of this text have succeeded in providing the user with not only practice assignments, but also solutions!

This unique approach will enable the DTP operator to check his/her end product - virtually a self-teach package.

The text comprises a series of practice assignments and adequate material is available for operators to practise, for example, page set-ups, print specifications etc. Groups of 4 assignments covering similar operations have been made available.

It is appreciated that users may be using different DTP packages but the aim remains the same - to produce text to a specified layout.

Operators and tutors should be aware that substitute print styles may be necessary depending upon availability.

This text will be invaluable for all potential DTP operators and will provide ample practice material for both operators and tutors.

ACKNOWLEDGEMENT

The authors would like to record their appreciation and thanks for the help and assistance given by their colleague Duncan Brown in the preparation of this text.

JAL/DCM

CHAIRMAN'S STATEMENT

> ASSIGNMENT 1
> Key in text below.
> Margins - 25 mm (no hyphenation at line endings).
> Top margin - 25 mm.
> Type Specifications - Helvetica 12 point.
> Auto leading.
> Print one copy. Save as ASS1.

INTRODUCTION

Last year has seen a remarkable growth in our business to the extent that we have increased our sales force by 5 per cent to cope with the increased demand for our product. In recent years the demand for vacations has increased - customers are now taking short breaks as well as the traditional summer vacations. Our Management Team has improved the service to the customers by offering a wide and varied selection of reasonably priced holidays and the customer has responded by demanding better accommodation, better meals and improved travel arrangements. All of these have been taken on board by the Management Team and this has resulted in an increase in sales in what must be considered to be "an expanding market".

RESULTS

I am pleased to report to our stockholders that earnings per share have increased by 28 per cent. This has enabled us to declare a final dividend of 3.55 pence, giving an overall increase for the year of 10.5 per cent. This increase is the highest for a number of years and it indicates the confidence which exists within our Company. We are determined to increase the efficiency of our activities within the Company over the next 3 years. Our Management Team is strong with many new proposals coming forward for a maintenance of our market position. We aim to target Short Breaks next year with the emphasis being on an improved option choice within Scotland. We also aim to improve the selection of European locations for both short and long stay holidays.

I am confident that we can exploit the growth opportunities which these offer.

BOARD

Two new Directors have been appointed recently. Mrs Hilary Whyte has extensive knowledge of European holidays and Mr John Black brings extensive experience and knowledge of the home market.

Mrs Marion Duncan and Mr James Clive retired from the Board and we wish them well in their retirement.

CHAIRMAN'S STATEMENT

INTRODUCTION

I am pleased to announce pre-tax profits for the year of £696 million. This is an increase of 6% on last year's figures. The post-tax figures for the current year have also shown a slight increase (1.5%) to £294 million which has covered the proposed dividend allowance for shareholders. As you will no doubt be aware the current market conditions, although slow, have improved and the prospects for next year appear to be brighter than first anticipated for our financial institution. Indeed, I would suggest that our organisation is in a much stronger position than many of our foreign competitors. This must be encouraging news for our shareholders and our customers alike.

Customers remain to be our top priority and this is reflected in the proposals and recommendations for the future as laid out in the Annual Report and Accounts.

BOARD

Since last year's report the Board have seen a number of changes. Two new members have been welcomed to the Board at Directorate level. Mr Kenneth McDonald joined us in November of last year as Senior Executive and Miss Eileen Fraser was appointed in February as Financial Controller (Foreign Investment). Mr Johnston Forsyth will be retiring at the forthcoming Annual General Meeting. Mr Forsyth joined the Board in 1976 and was Vice Chairman from 1981 to 1987. He has made a significant contribution to the organisation over many years, for which we, the Board are extremely grateful. I take this opportunity of wishing him a healthy and happy retirement.

STAFF

Our Management Staff have had a difficult year with the introduction of new management techniques. They have had to participate in many new aspects of organisational procedures and evaluation exercises over the last financial year. I am sure these new initiatives will be welcomed by staff at all levels in the very near future. On behalf of the Board I thank them for their continued effort and support.

HOME IMPROVEMENTS

> ASSIGNMENT 3
> Key in text below.
> Margins - 25 mm (no hyphenation at line endings).
> Top margin - 25 mm.
> Type specifications - Helvetica 12 point.
> Auto leading.
> Print one copy.   Save as ASS3.

Living Area

Great scope exists for the householder to improve the decor within the living areas of the home. Wall papering, painting, wood cladding, plastering and door replacement are all areas where the homeowner can make considerable savings both in time and money. Suppliers are only too willing to offer suggestions both in the method of construction and in the design of the living areas. This not only reassures the individual but also can save time and extra expense.

The quality of self-assembly furniture has given even wider scope for the individual and a wide range of furniture can be purchased and assembled using only the minimum of tools. In all self-assembly packs, the instructions are clear and concise.

Kitchen Area

Although many householders will engage professional help when installing a new kitchen, it is nevertheless possible to design and purchase units for the kitchen area from the DIY store. Considerable time and care should be taken, however, when measuring for wall units and cupboards. Problems can arise when wall measurements do not correspond to the unit sizes. Here again, however, the DIY enthusiast can undertake such a project knowing that expert advice and hints are readily available from the supplier.

Improving the kitchen is probably the most value-adding improvement which can be made within the home. Considering the amount of time spent in this area, it will also be one of the first areas of the home to be upgraded. Built-in or freestanding appliances can be costly additions to the kitchen but the majority of homes will have such appliances as the washing machine, tumble dryer, dishwasher, fridge or freezer and a microwave oven.

Bathroom Area

A replacement bathroom will be determined by not only your current needs, but also the likely future requirements for the area. Modern bathroom equipment is available from the DIY store in a wide choice of styles, shapes and colours. Planning the bathroom is critical since this can often be the smallest area in the home. Will the size and shape of the room allow for the installation of both a bath and a separate shower?

GOLF - "THE LYMAC WAY"

General Information

With the increasing amount of leisure time that is given to the general business community, it is important that this additional time is spent in a wise, healthy and enjoyable way. There's no better way to utilise this time than to participate in the art of "The Royal and Ancient Game". Lymac Golf and Leisure Promotion can offer a wide variety of options that will cater for all ages, male or female in the world of golf. Our aim is to provide our clients with the opportunity to play quality golf courses, obtain professional tuition, have fun and pleasure - all at affordable prices. We will also provide "off-the-course" entertainment for all of our clients, their families and guests while under contract with Lymac.

Courses

Lymac Golf and Leisure Promotion have acquired the reputation of being able to promote one of the largest selections of golf course availability to their clients. Over the last 15 years we have been able to achieve an unbeatable success rate in obtaining access to some of the most famous golfing links in a number of countries. Lymac concentrates its promotional activities at "the home of golf" - Scotland, but can also facilitate requests for other courses in the United Kingdom and indeed the remainder of Europe. As yet, we have not moved into the full international golfing arena, but plans are well ahead to enter into the United States of America in the next 2 years.

Leave the arrangements to us - we have the drive to book the course of your choice.

Equipment

Don't let the lack of equipment or difficulty of travel stand in your way - Lymac offer a full range of equipment-hire from a basic half-set of irons to tournament-grade clubs, bags, balls, trolleys and even electric "buggies" in your package. All the major suppliers of golf equipment are on contract with Lymac and we will guarantee to supply the equipment of your choice on request. We aim to please every golfer who registers with our firm and aim to make the choice of outing a time to remember.

If you want to be on par with the professionals - contact Lymac.

ASSIGNMENT 4
Key in text below.
Margins - 25 mm (no hyphenation at line endings).
Top margin - 25 mm.
Type specifications - Bookman 12 point.
Auto leading.
Print one copy. Save as ASS4.

CHAIRMAN'S STATEMENT

INTRODUCTION

Last year has seen a remarkable growth in our business to the extent that we have increased our sales force by 5 per cent to cope with the increased demand for our product. In recent years the demand for vacations has increased - customers are now taking short breaks as well as the traditional summer vacations. Our Management Team has improved the service to the customers by offering a wide and varied selection of reasonably priced holidays and the customer has responded by demanding better accommodation, better meals and improved travel arrangements. All of these have been taken on board by the Management Team and this has resulted in an increase in sales in what must be considered to be "an expanding market".

RESULTS

I am pleased to report to our stockholders that earnings per share have increased by 28 per cent. This has enabled us to declare a final dividend of 3.55 pence, giving an overall increase for the year of 10.5 per cent. This increase is the highest for a number of years and it indicates the confidence which exists within our Company. We are determined to increase the efficiency of our activities within the Company over the next 3 years. Our Management Team is strong with many new proposals coming forward for a maintenance of our market position. We aim to target Short Breaks next year with the emphasis being on an improved option choice within Scotland. We also aim to improve the selection of European locations for both short and long stay holidays.

I am confident that we can exploit the growth opportunities which these offer.

BOARD

Two new Directors have been appointed recently. Mrs Hilary Whyte has extensive knowledge of European holidays and Mr John Black brings extensive experience and knowledge of the home market.

Mrs Marion Duncan and Mr James Clive retired from the Board and we wish them well in their retirement.

CHAIRMAN'S STATEMENT

> ASSIGNMENT 6
> Recall ASS2 and make the alterations indicated.
> Change type specifications to Helvetica - Narrow.
> Change main heading to 18 point - embolden and italics.
> Change shoulder headings to 14 point.
> Change paragraph text to 14 point.
> Auto leading.
> Print one copy. Save as ASS6.

INTRODUCTION

I am pleased to announce pre-tax profits for the year of £696 million. This is an increase of 6% on last year's figures. The post-tax figures for the current year have also shown a slight increase (1.5%) to £294 million which has covered the proposed dividend allowance for shareholders. As you will no doubt be aware the current market conditions, although slow, have improved and the prospects for next year appear to be brighter than first anticipated for our financial institution. Indeed, I would suggest that our organisation is in a much stronger position than many of our foreign competitors. This must be encouraging news for our shareholders and our customers alike.

Customers remain to be our top priority and this is reflected in the proposals and recommendations for the future as laid out in the Annual Report and Accounts.

BOARD

Since last year's report the Board have seen a number of changes. Two new members have been welcomed to the Board. Mr Kenneth McDonald joined us in November of last year as Senior Executive and Miss Eileen Fraser was appointed in February as Financial Controller (Foreign Investment). Mr Johnston Forsyth will be retiring at the forthcoming Annual General Meeting. Mr Forsyth joined the Board in 1976 and was Vice Chairman from 1981 to 1987. He has made a significant contribution to the organisation over many years, for which we, the Board are extremely grateful. I take this opportunity of wishing him a healthy and happy retirement.

STAFF

Our Management Staff have had a difficult year with the introduction of new management techniques. They have had to participate in many new aspects of organisational procedures and evaluation exercises over the last financial year. I am sure these new initiatives will be welcomed by staff at all levels in the very near future. On behalf of the Board I thank them for their continued effort and support.

HOME IMPROVEMENTS

> ASSIGNMENT 7
> Recall ASS3 and make the alterations indicated.
> Change type specifications to Times Roman.
> Change main heading to 18 point and embolden.
> Change shoulder headings to 14 point.
> Change paragraph text to 14 point.
> Change leading to 14 point.
> Print one copy. Save as ASS7.

Living Area

Great scope exists for the householder to improve the decor within the living areas of the home. Wall papering, painting, wood cladding, plastering and door replacement are all areas where the homeowner can make considerable savings both in time and money. Suppliers are only too willing to offer suggestions both in the method of construction and in the design of the living areas. This not only reassures the individual but also can save time and extra expense.

The quality of self-assembly furniture has given even wider scope for the individual and a wide range of furniture can be purchased and assembled using only the minimum of tools. In all self-assembly packs, the instructions are clear and concise.

Kitchen Area

Although many householders will engage professional help when installing a new kitchen, it is nevertheless possible to design and purchase units for the kitchen area from the DIY store. Considerable time and care should be taken, however, when measuring for wall units and cupboards. Problems can arise when wall measurements do not correspond to the unit sizes. Here again, however, the DIY enthusiast can undertake such a project knowing that expert advice and hints are readily available from the supplier.

Improving the kitchen is probably the most value-adding improvement which can be made within the home. Considering the amount of time spent in this area, it will also be one of the first areas of the home to be upgraded. Built-in or freestanding appliances can be costly additions to the kitchen but the majority of homes will have such appliances as the washing machine, tumble dryer, dishwasher, fridge or freezer and a microwave oven.

Bathroom Area

A replacement bathroom will be determined by not only your current needs, but also the likely future requirements for the area. Modern bathroom equipment is available from the DIY store in a wide choice of styles, shapes and colours. Planning the bathroom is critical since this can often be the smallest area in the home. Will the size and shape of the room allow for the installation of both a bath and a separate shower?

GOLF - "THE LYMAC WAY"

> ASSIGNMENT 8
> Recall ASS4 and make the alterations indicated.
> Change type specifications to Helvetica - Narrow.
> Change main heading to 18 point - embolden and italics.
> Change shoulder headings to 14 point.
> Change paragraph text to 14 point.
> Auto leading.
> Print one copy. Save as ASS8.

General Information

With the increasing amount of leisure time that is given to the general business community, it is important that this additional time is spent in a wise, healthy and enjoyable way. There's no better way to utilise this time than to participate in the art of "The Royal and Ancient Game". Lymac Golf and Leisure Promotion can offer a wide variety of options that will cater for all ages, male or female in the world of golf. Our aim is to provide our clients with the opportunity to play quality golf courses, obtain professional tuition, have fun and pleasure - all at affordable prices. We will also provide "off-the-course" entertainment for all of our clients, their families and guests while under contract with Lymac.

Courses

Lymac Golf and Leisure Promotion have acquired the reputation of being able to promote one of the largest selections of golf course availability to their clients. Over the last 15 years we have been able to achieve an unbeatable success rate in obtaining access to some of the most famous golfing links in a number of countries. Lymac concentrates its promotional activities at "the home of golf" - Scotland, but can also facilitate requests for other courses in the United Kingdom and indeed the remainder of Europe. As yet, we have not moved into the full international golfing arena, but plans are well ahead to enter into the United States of America in the next 2 years.

Leave the arrangements to us - we have the drive to book the course of your choice.

Equipment

Don't let the lack of equipment or difficulty of travel stand in your way - Lymac offer a full range of equipment-hire from a basic half-set of irons to tournament-grade clubs, bags, balls, trolleys and even electric "buggies" in your package. All the major suppliers of golf equipment are on contract with Lymac and we will guarantee to supply the equipment of your choice on request. We aim to please every golfer who registers with our firm and aim to make the choice of outing a time to remember.

If you want to be on par with the professionals - contact Lymac.

CHAIRMAN'S STATEMENT

> ASSIGNMENT 9
> Recall ASS5 and make the alterations indicated.
> Change type specifications to Courier.
> Retain top margin of 25 mm for main heading (18 point).
> Retain 14 point for shoulder headings.
> Commence INTRODUCTION at 100 mm from top edge of paper.
> Change paragraph text to 8 point (Courier).
> Auto leading and Justify.
> Left and right margins - 30 mm.
> Print one copy. Save as ASS9.

INTRODUCTION

Last year has seen a remarkable growth in our business to the extent that we have increased our sales force by 5 per cent to cope with the increased demand for our product. In recent years the demand for vacations has increased - customers are now taking short breaks as well as the traditional summer vacations. Our Management Team has improved the service to the customers by offering a wide and varied selection of reasonably priced holidays and the customer has responded by demanding better accommodation, better meals and improved travel arrangements. All of these have been taken on board by the Management Team and this has resulted in an increase in sales in what must be considered to be "an expanding market".

RESULTS

I am pleased to report to our stockholders that earnings per share have increased by 28 per cent. This has enabled us to declare a final dividend of 3.55 pence, giving an overall increase for the year of 10.5 per cent. This increase is the highest for a number of years and it indicates the confidence which exists within our Company. We are determined to increase the efficiency of our activities within the Company over the next 3 years. Our Management Team is strong with many new proposals coming forward for a maintenance of our market position. We aim to target Short Breaks next year with the emphasis being on an improved option choice within Scotland. We also aim to improve the selection of European locations for both short and long stay holidays.

I am confident that we can exploit the growth opportunities which these offer.

BOARD

Two new Directors have been appointed recently. Mrs Hilary Whyte has extensive knowledge of European holidays and Mr John Black brings extensive experience and knowledge of the home market.

Mrs Marion Duncan and Mr James Clive retired from the Board and we wish them well in their retirement.

CHAIRMAN'S STATEMENT

> ASSIGNMENT 10
> Recall ASS6 and make the alterations indicated.
> Change type specifications to Helvetica.
> Retain top margin of 25 mm for main heading (18 point).
> Retain 14 point for shoulder headings.
> Commence INTRODUCTION at 110 mm from top edge of paper.
> Change paragraph text to 8 point (Helvetica).
> Auto leading and Justify.
> Left and right margins - 30 mm.
> Print one copy. Save as ASS10.

INTRODUCTION

I am pleased to announce pre-tax profits for the year of £696 million. This is an increase of 6% on last year's figures. The post-tax figures for the current year have also shown a slight increase (1.5%) to £294 million which has covered the proposed dividend allowance for shareholders. As you will no doubt be aware the current market conditions, although slow, have improved and the prospects for next year appear to be brighter than first anticipated for our financial institution. Indeed, I would suggest that our organisation is in a much stronger position than many of our foreign competitors. This must be encouraging news for our shareholders and our customers alike.

Customers remain to be our top priority and this is reflected in the proposals and recommendations for the future as laid out in the Annual Report and Accounts.

BOARD

Since last year's report the Board have seen a number of changes. Two new members have been welcomed to the Board. Mr Kenneth McDonald joined us in November of last year as Senior Executive and Miss Eileen Fraser was appointed in February as Financial Controller (Foreign Investment). Mr Johnston Forsyth will be retiring at the forthcoming Annual General Meeting. Mr Forsyth joined the Board in 1976 and was Vice Chairman from 1981 to 1987. He has made a significant contribution to the organisation over many years, for which we, the Board are extremely grateful. I take this opportunity of wishing him a healthy and happy retirement.

STAFF

Our Management Staff have had a difficult year with the introduction of new management techniques. They have had to participate in many new aspects of organisational procedures and evaluation exercises over the last financial year. I am sure these new initiatives will be welcomed by staff at all levels in the very near future. On behalf of the Board I thank them for their continued effort and support.

HOME IMPROVEMENTS

> ASSIGNMENT 11
> Recall ASS7 and make the alterations indicated.
> Change type specifications to Courier.
> Retain top margin of 25 mm for main heading (18 point).
> Retain 14 point for shoulder headings.
> Commence <u>Living Area</u> at 100 mm from top edge of paper.
> Change paragraph text to 8 point (Courier).
> Auto leading and Justify.
> Left and right margins - 30 mm.
> Print one copy. Save as ASS11.

Living Area

Great scope exists for the householder to improve the decor within the living areas of the home. Wall papering, painting, wood cladding, plastering and door replacement are all areas where the homeowner can make considerable savings both in time and money. Suppliers are only too willing to offer suggestions both in the method of construction and in the design of the living areas. This not only reassures the individual but also can save time and extra expense.

The quality of self-assembly furniture has given even wider scope for the individual and a wide range of furniture can be purchased and assembled using only the minimum of tools. In all self-assembly packs, the instructions are clear and concise.

Kitchen Area

Although many householders will engage professional help when installing a new kitchen, it is nevertheless possible to design and purchase units for the kitchen area from the DIY store. Considerable time and care should be taken, however, when measuring for wall units and cupboards. Problems can arise when wall measurements do not correspond to the unit sizes. Here again, however, the DIY enthusiast can undertake such a project knowing that expert advice and hints are readily available from the supplier.

Improving the kitchen is probably the most value-adding improvement which can be made within the home. Considering the amount of time spent in this area, it will also be one of the first areas of the home to be upgraded. Built-in or freestanding appliances can be costly additions to the kitchen but the majority of homes will have such appliances as the washing machine, tumble dryer, dishwasher, fridge or freezer and a microwave oven.

Bathroom Area

A replacement bathroom will be determined by not only your current needs, but also the likely future requirements for the area. Modern bathroom equipment is available from the DIY store in a wide choice of styles, shapes and colours. Planning the bathroom is critical since this can often be the smallest area in the home. Will the size and shape of the room allow for the installation of both a bath and a separate shower?

GOLF - "THE LYMAC WAY"

> ASSIGNMENT 12
> Recall ASS8 and make the alterations indicated.
> Change type specifications to Helvetica.
> Retain top margin of 25 mm for main heading (18 point).
> Retain 14 point for shoulder headings.
> Commence General Information at 110 mm from top edge of paper.
> Change paragraph text to 8 point (Helvetica).
> Auto leading and Justify.
> Left and right margins - 30 mm.
> Print one copy. Save as ASS12.

General Information

With the increasing amount of leisure time that is given to the general business community, it is important that this additional time is spent in a wise, healthy and enjoyable way. There's no better way to utilise this time than to participate in the art of "The Royal and Ancient Game". Lymac Golf and Leisure Promotion can offer a wide variety of options that will cater for all ages, male or female in the world of golf. Our aim is to provide our clients with the opportunity to play quality golf courses, obtain professional tuition, have fun and pleasure - all at affordable prices. We will also provide "off-the-course" entertainment for all of our clients, their families and guests while under contract with Lymac.

Courses

Lymac Golf and Leisure Promotion have acquired the reputation of being able to promote one of the largest selections of golf course availability to their clients. Over the last 15 years we have been able to achieve an unbeatable success rate in obtaining access to some of the most famous golfing links in a number of countries. Lymac concentrates its promotional activities at "the home of golf" - Scotland, but can also facilitate requests for other courses in the United Kingdom and indeed the remainder of Europe. As yet, we have not moved into the full international golfing arena, but plans are well ahead to enter into the United States of America in the next 2 years.

Leave the arrangements to us - we have the drive to book the course of your choice.

Equipment

Don't let the lack of equipment or difficulty of travel stand in your way - Lymac offer a full range of equipment-hire from a basic half-set of irons to tournament-grade clubs, bags, balls, trolleys and even electric "buggies" in your package. All the major suppliers of golf equipment are on contract with Lymac and we will guarantee to supply the equipment of your choice on request. We aim to please every golfer who registers with our firm and aim to make the choice of outing a time to remember.

If you want to be on par with the professionals - contact Lymac.

> ASSIGNMENT 13
> Recall ASS9 and make the alterations indicated.
> Text to be arranged in 2 columns - 70 mm wide; 20 mm space between.
> Top margin (before main heading) to be 60 mm.
> Bottom margin to be 40 mm. Commence INTRODUCTION at 80 mm from top edge of paper.
> Left and right margins - 25 mm.
> Change type specifications to AvantGarde.
> Main heading 14 point; shoulder headings 12 point; paragraph text 10 point.
> First line at top of column 2 should be in alignment with first line in column 1.
> Auto leading. Print one copy. Save as ASS13.

CHAIRMAN'S STATEMENT

INTRODUCTION

Last year has seen a remarkable growth in our business to the extent that we have increased our sales force by 5 per cent to cope with the increased demand for our product. In recent years the demand for vacations has increased - customers are now taking short breaks as well as the traditional summer vacations. Our Management Team has improved the service to the customers by offering a wide and varied selection of reasonably priced holidays and the customer has responded by demanding better accommodation, better meals and improved travel arrangements. All of these have been taken on board by the Management Team and this has resulted in an increase in sales in what must be considered to be "an expanding market".

RESULTS

I am pleased to report to our stockholders that earnings per share have increased by 28 per cent. This has enabled us to declare a final dividend of 3.55 pence, giving an overall increase for the year of 10.5 per cent. This increase is the highest for a number of years and it indicates the confidence which exists within our Company. We are determined to increase the efficiency of our activities within the Company over the next 3 years. Our Management Team is strong with many new proposals coming forward for a maintenance of our market position. We aim to target Short Breaks next year with the emphasis being on an improved option choice within Scotland. We also aim to improve the selection of European locations for both short and long stay holidays.

I am confident that we can exploit the growth opportunities which these offer.

BOARD

Two new Directors have been appointed recently. Mrs Hilary Whyte has extensive knowledge of European holidays and Mr John Black brings extensive experience and knowledge of the home market.

Mrs Marion Duncan and Mr James Clive retired from the Board and we wish them well in their retirement.

> ASSIGNMENT 14
> Recall ASS10 and make the alterations indicated.
> Text to be arranged in 2 columns - 75 mm wide; 10 mm space between.
> Top margin (before main heading) to be 70 mm.
> Commence INTRODUCTION at 10 mm below main heading.
> Left and right margins - 25 mm.
> Change type specifications to Palatino.
> Main heading 14 point; shoulder headings 12 point; paragraph text 10 point.
> Align STAFF with INTRODUCTION.
> Auto leading. Print one copy. Save as ASS14.

CHAIRMAN'S STATEMENT

INTRODUCTION

I am pleased to announce pre-tax profits for the year of £696 million. This is an increase of 6% on last year's figures. The post-tax figures for the current year have also shown a slight increase (1.5%) to £294 million which has covered the proposed dividend allowance for shareholders. As you will no doubt be aware the current market conditions, although slow, have improved and the prospects for next year appear to be brighter than first anticipated for our financial institution. Indeed, I would suggest that our organisation is in a much stronger position than many of our foreign competitors. This must be encouraging news for our shareholders and our customers alike.

Customers remain to be our top priority and this is reflected in the proposals and recommendations for the future as laid out in the Annual Report and Accounts.

BOARD

Since last year's report the Board have seen a number of changes. Two new members have been welcomed to the Board. Mr Kenneth McDonald joined us in November of last year as Senior Executive and Miss Eileen Fraser was appointed in February as Financial Controller (Foreign Investment). Mr Johnston Forsyth will be retiring at the forthcoming Annual General Meeting. Mr Forsyth joined the Board in 1976 and was Vice Chairman from 1981 to 1987. He has made a significant contribution to the organisation over many years, for which we, the Board are extremely grateful. I take this opportunity of wishing him a healthy and happy retirement.

STAFF

Our Management Staff have had a difficult year with the introduction of new management techniques. They have had to participate in many new aspects of organisational procedures and evaluation exercises over the last financial year. I am sure these new initiatives will be welcomed by staff at all levels in the very near future. On behalf of the Board I thank them for their continued effort and support.

> ASSIGNMENT 15
> Recall ASS11 and make the alterations indicated.
> Text to be arranged in 2 columns - 70 mm wide; 20 mm space between.
> Top margin (before main heading) to be 60 mm.
> Bottom margin to be 40 mm. Commence Living Area at 80 mm from top edge of paper.
> Left and right margins - 25 mm.
> Change type specifications to AvantGarde.
> Main heading 14 point; shoulder headings 12 point; paragraph text 10 point.
> First line at top of column 2 should be in alignment with first line in column 1.
> Auto leading. Print one copy. Save as ASS15.

HOME IMPROVEMENTS

Living Area

Great scope exists for the householder to improve the decor within the living areas of the home. Wall papering, painting, wood cladding, plastering and door replacement are all areas where the homeowner can make considerable savings both in time and money. Suppliers are only too willing to offer suggestions both in the method of construction and in the design of the living areas. This not only reassures the individual but also can save time and extra expense.

The quality of self-assembly furniture has given even wider scope for the individual and a wide range of furniture can be purchased and assembled using only the minimum of tools. In all self-assembly packs, the instructions are clear and concise.

Kitchen Area

Although many householders will engage professional help when installing a new kitchen, it is nevertheless possible to design and purchase units for the kitchen area from the DIY store. Considerable time and care should be taken, however, when measuring for wall units and cupboards. Problems can arise when wall measurements do not correspond to the unit sizes. Here again, however, the DIY enthusiast can undertake such a project knowing that expert advice and hints are readily available from the supplier.

Improving the kitchen is probably the most value-adding improvement which can be made within the home. Considering the amount of time spent in this area, it will also be one of the first areas of the home to be upgraded. Built-in or freestanding appliances can be costly additions to the kitchen but the majority of homes will have such appliances as the washing machine, tumble dryer, dishwasher, fridge or freezer and a microwave oven.

Bathroom Area

A replacement bathroom will be determined by not only your current needs, but also the likely future requirements for the area. Modern bathroom equipment is available from the DIY store in a wide choice of styles, shapes and colours. Planning the bathroom is critical since this can often be the smallest area in the home. Will the size and shape of the room allow for the installation of both a bath and a separate shower?

> ASSIGNMENT 16
> Recall ASS12 and make the alterations indicated.
> Text to be arranged in 2 columns - 75 mm wide; 10 mm space between.
> Top margin (before main heading) to be 70 mm.
> Commence General Information at 10 mm below main heading.
> Left and right margins - 25 mm.
> Change type specifications to Palatino.
> Main heading 14 point; shoulder headings 12 point; paragraph text 10 point.
> Align Equipment with General Information.
> Auto leading. Print one copy. Save as ASS16.

GOLF - "THE LYMAC WAY"

General Information

With the increasing amount of leisure time that is given to the general business community, it is important that this additional time is spent in a wise, healthy and enjoyable way. There's no better way to utilise this time than to participate in the art of "The Royal and Ancient Game". Lymac Golf and Leisure Promotion can offer a wide variety of options that will cater for all ages, male or female in the world of golf. Our aim is to provide our clients with the opportunity to play quality golf courses, obtain professional tuition, have fun and pleasure - all at affordable prices. We will also provide "off-the-course" entertainment for all of our clients, their families and guests while under contract with Lymac.

Courses

Lymac Golf and Leisure Promotion have acquired the reputation of being able to promote one of the largest selections of golf course availability to their clients. Over the last 15 years we have been able to achieve an unbeatable success rate in obtaining access to some of the most famous golfing links in a number of countries. Lymac concentrates its promotional activities at "the home of golf" - Scotland, but can also facilitate requests for other courses in the United Kingdom and indeed the remainder of Europe. As yet, we have not moved into the full international golfing arena, but plans are well ahead to enter into the United States of America in the next 2 years.

Leave the arrangements to us - we have the drive to book the course of your choice.

Equipment

Don't let the lack of equipment or difficulty of travel stand in your way - Lymac offer a full range of equipment-hire from a basic half-set of irons to tournament-grade clubs, bags, balls, trolleys and even electric "buggies" in your package. All the major suppliers of golf equipment are on contract with Lymac and we will guarantee to supply the equipment of your choice on request. We aim to please every golfer who registers with our firm and aim to make the choice of outing a time to remember.

If you want to be on par with the professionals - contact Lymac.

> ASSIGNMENT 17
> Recall ASS13 and make the alterations indicated.
> Retain type specifications as in Assignment 13.
> Insert 3 vertical lines - 1 point.
> Left vertical line to be 10 mm before left column.
> Right vertical line to be 10 mm after right column.
> Central vertical line to be in centre of space between columns.
> Vertical lines to commence and end in line with paragraph text in column 1.
> Print one copy. Save as ASS17.

CHAIRMAN'S STATEMENT

INTRODUCTION

Last year has seen a remarkable growth in our business to the extent that we have increased our sales force by 5 per cent to cope with the increased demand for our product. In recent years the demand for vacations has increased - customers are now taking short breaks as well as the traditional summer vacations. Our Management Team has improved the service to the customers by offering a wide and varied selection of reasonably priced holidays and the customer has responded by demanding better accommodation, better meals and improved travel arrangements. All of these have been taken on board by the Management Team and this has resulted in an increase in sales in what must be considered to be "an expanding market".

RESULTS

I am pleased to report to our stockholders that earnings per share have increased by 28 per cent. This has enabled us to declare a final dividend of 3.55 pence, giving an overall increase for the year of 10.5 per cent. This increase is the highest for a number of years and it indicates the confidence which exists within our Company. We are determined to increase the efficiency of our activities within the Company over the next 3 years. Our Management Team is strong with many new proposals coming forward for a maintenance of our market position. We aim to target Short Breaks next year with the emphasis being on an improved option choice within Scotland. We also aim to improve the selection of European locations for both short and long stay holidays.

I am confident that we can exploit the growth opportunities which these offer.

BOARD

Two new Directors have been appointed recently. Mrs Hilary Whyte has extensive knowledge of European holidays and Mr John Black brings extensive experience and knowledge of the home market.

Mrs Marion Duncan and Mr James Clive retired from the Board and we wish them well in their retirement.

> ASSIGNMENT 18
> Recall ASS14 and make the alterations indicated.
> Retain type specifications as in Assignment 14.
> Insert 3 vertical lines - 2 point.
> Left vertical line to be 5 mm before left column.
> Right vertical line to be 5 mm after right column.
> Central vertical line to be in centre of space between columns.
> Vertical lines to commence and end in line with paragraph text in column 1.
> Print one copy. Save as ASS18.

CHAIRMAN'S STATEMENT

INTRODUCTION

I am pleased to announce pre-tax profits for the year of £696 million. This is an increase of 6% on last year's figures. The post-tax figures for the current year have also shown a slight increase (1.5%) to £294 million which has covered the proposed dividend allowance for shareholders. As you will no doubt be aware the current market conditions, although slow, have improved and the prospects for next year appear to be brighter than first anticipated for our financial institution. Indeed, I would suggest that our organisation is in a much stronger position than many of our foreign competitors. This must be encouraging news for our shareholders and our customers alike.

Customers remain to be our top priority and this is reflected in the proposals and recommendations for the future as laid out in the Annual Report and Accounts.

BOARD

Since last year's report the Board have seen a number of changes. Two new members have been welcomed to the Board. Mr Kenneth McDonald joined us in November of last year as Senior Executive and Miss Eileen Fraser was appointed in February as Financial Controller (Foreign Investment). Mr Johnston Forsyth will be retiring at the forthcoming Annual General Meeting. Mr Forsyth joined the Board in 1976 and was Vice Chairman from 1981 to 1987. He has made a significant contribution to the organisation over many years, for which we, the Board are extremely grateful. I take this opportunity of wishing him a healthy and happy retirement.

STAFF

Our Management Staff have had a difficult year with the introduction of new management techniques. They have had to participate in many new aspects of organisational procedures and evaluation exercises over the last financial year. I am sure these new initiatives will be welcomed by staff at all levels in the very near future. On behalf of the Board I thank them for their continued effort and support.

> ASSIGNMENT 19
> Recall ASS15 and make the alterations indicated.
> Retain type specifications as in Assignment 15.
> Insert 3 vertical lines - 1 point.
> Left vertical line to be 10 mm before left column.
> Right vertical line to be 10 mm after right column.
> Central vertical line to be in centre of space between columns.
> Vertical lines to commence and end in line with paragraph text in column 1.
> Print one copy. Save as ASS19.

HOME IMPROVEMENTS

Living Area

Great scope exists for the householder to improve the decor within the living areas of the home. Wall papering, painting, wood cladding, plastering and door replacement are all areas where the homeowner can make considerable savings both in time and money. Suppliers are only too willing to offer suggestions both in the method of construction and in the design of the living areas. This not only reassures the individual but also can save time and extra expense.

The quality of self-assembly furniture has given even wider scope for the individual and a wide range of furniture can be purchased and assembled using only the minimum of tools. In all self-assembly packs, the instructions are clear and concise.

Kitchen Area

Although many householders will engage professional help when installing a new kitchen, it is nevertheless possible to design and purchase units for the kitchen area from the DIY store. Considerable time and care should be taken, however, when measuring for wall units and cupboards. Problems can arise when wall measurements do not correspond to the unit sizes. Here again, however, the DIY enthusiast can undertake such a project knowing that expert advice and hints are readily available from the supplier.

Improving the kitchen is probably the most value-adding improvement which can be made within the home. Considering the amount of time spent in this area, it will also be one of the first areas of the home to be upgraded. Built-in or freestanding appliances can be costly additions to the kitchen but the majority of homes will have such appliances as the washing machine, tumble dryer, dishwasher, fridge or freezer and a microwave oven.

Bathroom Area

A replacement bathroom will be determined by not only your current needs, but also the likely future requirements for the area. Modern bathroom equipment is available from the DIY store in a wide choice of styles, shapes and colours. Planning the bathroom is critical since this can often be the smallest area in the home. Will the size and shape of the room allow for the installation of both a bath and a separate shower?

> ASSIGNMENT 20
> Recall ASS16 and make the alterations indicated.
> Retain type specifications as in Assignment 16.
> Insert 3 vertical lines - 2 point.
> Left vertical line to be 5 mm before left column.
> Right vertical line to be 5 mm after right column.
> Central vertical line to be in centre of space between columns.
> Vertical lines to commence and end in line with paragraph text in column 1.
> Print one copy. Save as ASS20.

GOLF - "THE LYMAC WAY"

General Information

With the increasing amount of leisure time that is given to the general business community, it is important that this additional time is spent in a wise, healthy and enjoyable way. There's no better way to utilise this time than to participate in the art of "The Royal and Ancient Game". Lymac Golf and Leisure Promotion can offer a wide variety of options that will cater for all ages, male or female in the world of golf. Our aim is to provide our clients with the opportunity to play quality golf courses, obtain professional tuition, have fun and pleasure - all at affordable prices. We will also provide "off-the-course" entertainment for all of our clients, their families and guests while under contract with Lymac.

Courses

Lymac Golf and Leisure Promotion have acquired the reputation of being able to promote one of the largest selections of golf course availability to their clients. Over the last 15 years we have been able to achieve an unbeatable success rate in obtaining access to some of the most famous golfing links in a number of countries. Lymac concentrates its promotional activities at "the home of golf" - Scotland, but can also facilitate requests for other courses in the United Kingdom and indeed the remainder of Europe. As yet, we have not moved into the full international golfing arena, but plans are well ahead to enter into the United States of America in the next 2 years.

Leave the arrangements to us - we have the drive to book the course of your choice.

Equipment

Don't let the lack of equipment or difficulty of travel stand in your way - Lymac offer a full range of equipment-hire from a basic half-set of irons to tournament-grade clubs, bags, balls, trolleys and even electric "buggies" in your package. All the major suppliers of golf equipment are on contract with Lymac and we will guarantee to supply the equipment of your choice on request. We aim to please every golfer who registers with our firm and aim to make the choice of outing a time to remember.

If you want to be on par with the professionals - contact Lymac.

> ASSIGNMENT 21
> Recall ASS17 and make the alterations indicated.
> Insert box (70 mm x 80 mm) - 1 point - in left column after the main heading. Commence at 80 mm from top edge of paper.
> INTRODUCTION (and following text) to commence 170 mm from top edge of paper.
> Vertical lines to commence 80 mm from top edge of paper.
> Vertical lines to end in alignment with text in column 1.
> RESULTS section (and following text) to commence 80 mm from top edge of paper.
> Change leading to 10 point. Print one copy. Save as ASS21.

CHAIRMAN'S STATEMENT

INTRODUCTION

Last year has seen a remarkable growth in our business to the extent that we have increased our sales force by 5 per cent to cope with the increased demand for our product. In recent years the demand for vacations has increased - customers are now taking short breaks as well as the traditional summer vacations. Our Management Team has improved the service to the customers by offering a wide and varied selection of reasonably priced holidays and the customer has responded by demanding better accommodation, better meals and improved travel arrangements. All of these have been taken on board by the Management Team and this has resulted in an increase in sales in what must be considered to be "an expanding market".

RESULTS

I am pleased to report to our stockholders that earnings per share have increased by 28 per cent. This has enabled us to declare a final dividend of 3.55 pence, giving an overall increase for the year of 10.5 per cent. This increase is the highest for a number of years and it indicates the confidence which exists within our Company. We are determined to increase the efficiency of our activities within the Company over the next 3 years. Our Management Team is strong with many new proposals coming forward for a maintenance of our market position. We aim to target Short Breaks next year with the emphasis being on an improved option choice within Scotland. We also aim to improve the selection of European locations for both short and long stay holidays.

I am confident that we can exploit the growth opportunities which these offer.

BOARD

Two new Directors have been appointed recently. Mrs Hilary Whyte has extensive knowledge of European holidays and Mr John Black brings extensive experience and knowledge of the home market.

Mrs Marion Duncan and Mr James Clive retired from the Board and we wish them well in their retirement.

> ASSIGNMENT 22
> Recall ASS18 and make the alterations indicated.
> Insert box (75 mm x 90 mm) - 2 point - in left column
> after the main heading. Commence at 80 mm from top edge
> of paper.
> INTRODUCTION (and following text) to commence
> 10 mm below bottom edge of box.
> Text in column 2 should commence 80 mm from top edge of paper.
> Vertical lines to commence 80 mm from top edge of paper.
> Vertical lines to end in alignment with text in column 1.
> Change leading to 12 point. Print one copy. Save as ASS22.

CHAIRMAN'S STATEMENT

INTRODUCTION

I am pleased to announce pre-tax profits for the year of £696 million. This is an increase of 6% on last year's figures. The post-tax figures for the current year have also shown a slight increase (1.5%) to £294 million which has covered the proposed dividend allowance for shareholders. As you will no doubt be aware the current market conditions, although slow, have improved and the prospects for next year appear to be brighter than first anticipated for our financial institution. Indeed, I would suggest that our organisation is in a much stronger position than many of our foreign competitors. This must be encouraging news for our shareholders and our customers alike.

Customers remain to be our top priority and this is reflected in the proposals and recommendations for the future as laid out in the Annual Report and Accounts.

BOARD

Since last year's report the Board have seen a number of changes. Two new members have been welcomed to the Board. Mr Kenneth McDonald joined us in November of last year as Senior Executive and Miss Eileen Fraser was appointed in February as Financial Controller (Foreign Investment). Mr Johnston Forsyth will be retiring at the forthcoming Annual General Meeting. Mr Forsyth joined the Board in 1976 and was Vice Chairman from 1981 to 1987. He has made a significant contribution to the organisation over many years, for which we, the Board are extremely grateful. I take this opportunity of wishing him a healthy and happy retirement.

STAFF

Our Management Staff have had a difficult year with the introduction of new management techniques. They have had to participate in many new aspects of organisational procedures and evaluation exercises over the last financial year. I am sure these new initiatives will be welcomed by staff at all levels in the very near future. On behalf of the Board I thank them for their continued effort and support.

> ASSIGNMENT 23
> Recall ASS19 and make the alterations indicated.
> Insert box (70 mm x 80 mm) - 1 point - in left column after the main heading. Commence at 80 mm from top edge of paper.
> Living Area (and following text) to commence 170 mm from top edge of paper.
> Vertical lines to commence 80 mm from top edge of paper.
> Vertical lines to end in alignment with text in Column 1.
> Kitchen Area section (and following text) to commence 80 mm from top edge of paper.
> Change leading to 10 point. Print one copy. Save as ASS23.

HOME IMPROVEMENTS

Living Area

Great scope exists for the householder to improve the decor within the living areas of the home. Wall papering, painting, wood cladding, plastering and door replacement are all areas where the homeowner can make considerable savings both in time and money. Suppliers are only too willing to offer suggestions both in the method of construction and in the design of the living areas. This not only reassures the individual but also can save time and extra expense.

The quality of self-assembly furniture has given even wider scope for the individual and a wide range of furniture can be purchased and assembled using only the minimum of tools. In all self-assembly packs, the instructions are clear and concise.

Kitchen Area

Although many householders will engage professional help when installing a new kitchen, it is nevertheless possible to design and purchase units for the kitchen area from the DIY store. Considerable time and care should be taken, however, when measuring for wall units and cupboards. Problems can arise when wall measurements do not correspond to the unit sizes. Here again, however, the DIY enthusiast can undertake such a project knowing that expert advice and hints are readily available from the supplier.

Improving the kitchen is probably the most value-adding improvement which can be made within the home. Considering the amount of time spent in this area, it will also be one of the first areas of the home to be upgraded. Built-in or freestanding appliances can be costly additions to the kitchen but the majority of homes will have such appliances as the washing machine, tumble dryer, dishwasher, fridge or freezer and a microwave oven.

Bathroom Area

A replacement bathroom will be determined by not only your current needs, but also the likely future requirements for the area. Modern bathroom equipment is available from the DIY store in a wide choice of styles, shapes and colours. Planning the bathroom is critical since this can often be the smallest area in the home. Will the size and shape of the room allow for the installation of both a bath and a separate shower?

> ASSIGNMENT 24
> Recall ASS20 and make the alterations indicated.
> Insert box (75 mm x 90 mm) - 0.5 point - in left column after the main heading. Commence at 80 mm from top edge of paper.
> General Information (and following text) to commence 10 mm below bottom edge of box.
> Text in column 2 should commence 80 mm from top edge of paper.
> Vertical lines to commence 80 mm from top edge of paper.
> Vertical lines to end in alignment with text in column 1.
> Change leading to 12 point. Print one copy. Save as ASS24.

GOLF - "THE LYMAC WAY"

General Information

With the increasing amount of leisure time that is given to the general business community, it is important that this additional time is spent in a wise, healthy and enjoyable way. There's no better way to utilise this time than to participate in the art of "The Royal and Ancient Game". Lymac Golf and Leisure Promotion can offer a wide variety of options that will cater for all ages, male or female in the world of golf. Our aim is to provide our clients with the opportunity to play quality golf courses, obtain professional tuition, have fun and pleasure - all at affordable prices. We will also provide "off-the-course" entertainment for all of our clients, their families and guests while under contract with Lymac.

Courses

Lymac Golf and Leisure Promotion have acquired the reputation of being able to promote one of the largest selections of golf course availability to their clients. Over the last 15 years we have been able to achieve an unbeatable success rate in obtaining access to some of the most famous golfing links in a number of countries. Lymac concentrates its promotional activities at "the home of golf" - Scotland, but can also facilitate requests for other courses in the United Kingdom and indeed the remainder of Europe. As yet, we have not moved into the full international golfing arena, but plans are well ahead to enter into the United States of America in the next 2 years.

Leave the arrangements to us - we have the drive to book the course of your choice.

Equipment

Don't let the lack of equipment or difficulty of travel stand in your way - Lymac offer a full range of equipment-hire from a basic half-set of irons to tournament-grade clubs, bags, balls, trolleys and even electric "buggies" in your package. All the major suppliers of golf equipment are on contract with Lymac and we will guarantee to supply the equipment of your choice on request. We aim to please every golfer who registers with our firm and aim to make the choice of outing a time to remember.

If you want to be on par with the professionals - contact Lymac.

A & D TOURS PLC - Chairman's Statement

CHAIRMAN'S STATEMENT

> ASSIGNMENT 25
> Recall ASS21 and make the alterations indicated.
> Insert the header (12 point AvantGarde) as shown (in italics) 10 mm from top edge of paper.
> Lines (0.5 point) to begin and end in alignment with vertical lines.
> Vertical space between lines to be 15 mm.
> Print one copy. Save as ASS25.

INTRODUCTION

Last year has seen a remarkable growth in our business to the extent that we have increased our sales force by 5 per cent to cope with the increased demand for our product. In recent years the demand for vacations has increased - customers are now taking short breaks as well as the traditional summer vacations. Our Management Team has improved the service to the customers by offering a wide and varied selection of reasonably priced holidays and the customer has responded by demanding better accommodation, better meals and improved travel arrangements. All of these have been taken on board by the Management Team and this has resulted in an increase in sales in what must be considered to be "an expanding market".

RESULTS

I am pleased to report to our stockholders that earnings per share have increased by 28 per cent. This has enabled us to declare a final dividend of 3.55 pence, giving an overall increase for the year of 10.5 per cent. This increase is the highest for a number of years and it indicates the confidence which exists within our Company. We are determined to increase the efficiency of our activities within the Company over the next 3 years. Our Management Team is strong with many new proposals coming forward for a maintenance of our market position. We aim to target Short Breaks next year with the emphasis being on an improved option choice within Scotland. We also aim to improve the selection of European locations for both short and long stay holidays.

I am confident that we can exploit the growth opportunities which these offer.

BOARD

Two new Directors have been appointed recently. Mrs Hilary Whyte has extensive knowledge of European holidays and Mr John Black brings extensive experience and knowledge of the home market.

Mrs Marion Duncan and Mr James Clive retired from the Board and we wish them well in their retirement.

ALDON FINANCIAL SERVICES PLC - Chairman's Statement

> ASSIGNMENT 26
> Recall ASS22 and make the alterations indicated.
> Insert the header (12 point Palatino) as shown (embolden) 10 mm from top edge of paper.
> Lines (1 point) to begin and end in alignment with vertical lines.
> Vertical space between lines to be 13 mm.
> Print one copy. Save as ASS26.

CHAIRMAN'S STATEMENT

INTRODUCTION

I am pleased to announce pre-tax profits for the year of £696 million. This is an increase of 6% on last year's figures. The post-tax figures for the current year have also shown a slight increase (1.5%) to £294 million which has covered the proposed dividend allowance for shareholders. As you will no doubt be aware the current market conditions, although slow, have improved and the prospects for next year appear to be brighter than first anticipated for our financial institution. Indeed, I would suggest that our organisation is in a much stronger position than many of our foreign competitors. This must be encouraging news for our shareholders and our customers alike.

Customers remain to be our top priority and this is reflected in the proposals and recommendations for the future as laid out in the Annual Report and Accounts.

BOARD

Since last year's report the Board have seen a number of changes. Two new members have been welcomed to the Board. Mr Kenneth McDonald joined us in November of last year as Senior Executive and Miss Eileen Fraser was appointed in February as Financial Controller (Foreign Investment). Mr Johnston Forsyth will be retiring at the forthcoming Annual General Meeting. Mr Forsyth joined the Board in 1976 and was Vice Chairman from 1981 to 1987. He has made a significant contribution to the organisation over many years, for which we, the Board are extremely grateful. I take this opportunity of wishing him a healthy and happy retirement.

STAFF

Our Management Staff have had a difficult year with the introduction of new management techniques. They have had to participate in many new aspects of organisational procedures and evaluation exercises over the last financial year. I am sure these new initiatives will be welcomed by staff at all levels in the very near future. On behalf of the Board I thank them for their continued effort and support.

DDA STORES PLC - The Impact of DO IT YOURSELF

HOME IMPROVEMENTS

> ASSIGNMENT 27
> Recall ASS23 and make the alterations indicated.
> Insert the header (12 point AvantGarde) as shown (in italics)
> 10 mm from top edge of paper.
> Lines (0.5 point) to begin and end in alignment with vertical lines.
> Vertical space between lines to be 15 mm.
> Print one copy. Save as ASS27.

Living Area

Great scope exists for the householder to improve the decor within the living areas of the home. Wall papering, painting, wood cladding, plastering and door replacement are all areas where the homeowner can make considerable savings both in time and money. Suppliers are only too willing to offer suggestions both in the method of construction and in the design of the living areas. This not only reassures the individual but also can save time and extra expense.

The quality of self-assembly furniture has given even wider scope for the individual and a wide range of furniture can be purchased and assembled using only the minimum of tools. In all self-assembly packs, the instructions are clear and concise.

Kitchen Area

Although many householders will engage professional help when installing a new kitchen, it is nevertheless possible to design and purchase units for the kitchen area from the DIY store. Considerable time and care should be taken, however, when measuring for wall units and cupboards. Problems can arise when wall measurements do not correspond to the unit sizes. Here again, however, the DIY enthusiast can undertake such a project knowing that expert advice and hints are readily available from the supplier.

Improving the kitchen is probably the most value-adding improvement which can be made within the home. Considering the amount of time spent in this area, it will also be one of the first areas of the home to be upgraded. Built-in or freestanding appliances can be costly additions to the kitchen but the majority of homes will have such appliances as the washing machine, tumble dryer, dishwasher, fridge or freezer and a microwave oven.

Bathroom Area

A replacement bathroom will be determined by not only your current needs, but also the likely future requirements for the area. Modern bathroom equipment is available from the DIY store in a wide choice of styles, shapes and colours. Planning the bathroom is critical since this can often be the smallest area in the home. Will the size and shape of the room allow for the installation of both a bath and a separate shower?

LYMAC Golf and Leisure Promotion

> ASSIGNMENT 28
> Recall ASS24 and make the alterations indicated.
> Insert the header (12 point Palatino) as shown (embolden) 10 mm from top edge of paper.
> Lines (1 point) to begin and end in alignment with vertical lines.
> Vertical space between lines to be 13 mm.
> Print one copy. Save as ASS28.

GOLF - "THE LYMAC WAY"

General Information

With the increasing amount of leisure time that is given to the general business community, it is important that this additional time is spent in a wise, healthy and enjoyable way. There's no better way to utilise this time than to participate in the art of "The Royal and Ancient Game". Lymac Golf and Leisure Promotion can offer a wide variety of options that will cater for all ages, male or female in the world of golf. Our aim is to provide our clients with the opportunity to play quality golf courses, obtain professional tuition, have fun and pleasure - all at affordable prices. We will also provide "off-the-course" entertainment for all of our clients, their families and guests while under contract with Lymac.

Courses

Lymac Golf and Leisure Promotion have acquired the reputation of being able to promote one of the largest selections of golf course availability to their clients. Over the last 15 years we have been able to achieve an unbeatable success rate in obtaining access to some of the most famous golfing links in a number of countries. Lymac concentrates its promotional activities at "the home of golf" - Scotland, but can also facilitate requests for other courses in the United Kingdom and indeed the remainder of Europe. As yet, we have not moved into the full international golfing arena, but plans are well ahead to enter into the United States of America in the next 2 years.

Leave the arrangements to us - we have the drive to book the course of your choice.

Equipment

Don't let the lack of equipment or difficulty of travel stand in your way - Lymac offer a full range of equipment-hire from a basic half-set of irons to tournament-grade clubs, bags, balls, trolleys and even electric "buggies" in your package. All the major suppliers of golf equipment are on contract with Lymac and we will guarantee to supply the equipment of your choice on request. We aim to please every golfer who registers with our firm and aim to make the choice of outing a time to remember.

If you want to be on par with the professionals - contact Lymac.

> ASSIGNMENT 29
> Recall ASS5 and make the alterations indicated.
> At 40 mm from top edge of paper, insert a box 160 x 80 mm.
> Select 1 point line.
> Move text 10 mm below box.
> Change type specifications to Times Roman 10 point.
> Print one copy. Save as ASS29.

CHAIRMAN'S STATEMENT

INTRODUCTION

Last year has seen a remarkable growth in our business to the extent that we have increased our sales force by 5 per cent to cope with the increased demand for our product. In recent years the demand for vacations has increased - customers are now taking short breaks as well as the traditional summer vacations. Our Management Team has improved the service to the customers by offering a wide and varied selection of reasonably priced holidays and the customer has responded by demanding better accommodation, better meals and improved travel arrangements. All of these have been taken on board by the Management Team and this has resulted in an increase in sales in what must be considered to be "an expanding market".

RESULTS

I am pleased to report to our stockholders that earnings per share have increased by 28 per cent. This has enabled us to declare a final dividend of 3.55 pence, giving an overall increase for the year of 10.5 per cent. This increase is the highest for a number of years and it indicates the confidence which exists within our Company. We are determined to increase the efficiency of our activities within the Company over the next 3 years. Our Management Team is strong with many new proposals coming forward for a maintenance of our market position. We aim to target Short Breaks next year with the emphasis being on an improved option choice within Scotland. We also aim to improve the selection of European locations for both short and long stay holidays.

I am confident that we can exploit the growth opportunities which these offer.

BOARD

Two new Directors have been appointed recently. Mrs Hilary Whyte has extensive knowledge of European holidays and Mr John Black brings extensive experience and knowledge of the home market.

Mrs Marion Duncan and Mr James Clive retired from the Board and we wish them well in their retirement.

> ASSIGNMENT 30
> Recall ASS6 and make the alterations indicated.
> At 30 mm from top edge of paper, insert a box 160 x 75 mm.
> Select 0.5 point line.
> Move text 25 mm below box.
> Change type specifications to Helvetica 10 point.
> Main heading - remove italics.
> Print one copy. Save as ASS30.

CHAIRMAN'S STATEMENT

INTRODUCTION

I am pleased to announce pre-tax profits for the year of £696 million. This is an increase of 6% on last year's figures. The post-tax figures for the current year have also shown a slight increase (1.5%) to £294 million which has covered the proposed dividend allowance for shareholders. As you will no doubt be aware the current market conditions, although slow, have improved and the prospects for next year appear to be brighter than first anticipated for our financial institution. Indeed, I would suggest that our organisation is in a much stronger position than many of our foreign competitors. This must be encouraging news for our shareholders and our customers alike.

Customers remain to be our top priority and this is reflected in the proposals and recommendations for the future as laid out in the Annual Report and Accounts.

BOARD

Since last year's report the Board have seen a number of changes. Two new members have been welcomed to the Board. Mr Kenneth McDonald joined us in November of last year as Senior Executive and Miss Eileen Fraser was appointed in February as Financial Controller (Foreign Investment). Mr Johnston Forsyth will be retiring at the forthcoming Annual General Meeting. Mr Forsyth joined the Board in 1976 and was Vice Chairman from 1981 to 1987. He has made a significant contribution to the organisation over many years, for which we, the Board are extremely grateful. I take this opportunity of wishing him a healthy and happy retirement.

STAFF

Our Management Staff have had a difficult year with the introduction of new management techniques. They have had to participate in many new aspects of organisational procedures and evaluation exercises over the last financial year. I am sure these new initiatives will be welcomed by staff at all levels in the very near future. On behalf of the Board I thank them for their continued effort and support.

> ASSIGNMENT 31
> Recall ASS7 and make the alterations indicated.
> At 40 mm from top edge of paper, insert a box 160 x 80 mm.
> Select 1 point line.
> Move text 10 mm below box.
> Change type specifications to Times Roman 10 point.
> Bottom margin to be 20 mm.
> Print one copy. Save as ASS31.

HOME IMPROVEMENTS

Living Area

Great scope exists for the householder to improve the decor within the living areas of the home. Wall papering, painting, wood cladding, plastering and door replacement are all areas where the homeowner can make considerable savings both in time and money. Suppliers are only too willing to offer suggestions both in the method of construction and in the design of the living areas. This not only reassures the individual but also can save time and extra expense.

The quality of self-assembly furniture has given even wider scope for the individual and a wide range of furniture can be purchased and assembled using only the minimum of tools. In all self-assembly packs, the instructions are clear and concise.

Kitchen Area

Although many householders will engage professional help when installing a new kitchen, it is nevertheless possible to design and purchase units for the kitchen area from the DIY store. Considerable time and care should be taken, however, when measuring for wall units and cupboards. Problems can arise when wall measurements do not correspond to the unit sizes. Here again, however, the DIY enthusiast can undertake such a project knowing that expert advice and hints are readily available from the supplier.

Improving the kitchen is probably the most value-adding improvement which can be made within the home. Considering the amount of time spent in this area, it will also be one of the first areas of the home to be upgraded. Built-in or freestanding appliances can be costly additions to the kitchen but the majority of homes will have such appliances as the washing machine, tumble dryer, dishwasher, fridge or freezer and a microwave oven.

Bathroom Area

A replacement bathroom will be determined by not only your current needs, but also the likely future requirements for the area. Modern bathroom equipment is available from the DIY store in a wide choice of styles, shapes and colours. Planning the bathroom is critical since this can often be the smallest area in the home. Will the size and shape of the room allow for the installation of both a bath and a separate shower?

ASSIGNMENT 32
Recall ASS8 and make the alterations indicated.
At 30 mm from top edge of paper, insert a box 160 x 75 mm.
Select 0.5 point line.
Move text 25 mm below box.
Change type specifications to Helvetica 10 point.
Main heading - remove italics.
Bottom margin to be 20 mm.
Print one copy. Save as ASS32.

GOLF - "THE LYMAC WAY"

General Information

With the increasing amount of leisure time that is given to the general business community, it is important that this additional time is spent in a wise, healthy and enjoyable way. There's no better way to utilise this time than to participate in the art of "The Royal and Ancient Game". Lymac Golf and Leisure Promotion can offer a wide variety of options that will cater for all ages, male or female in the world of golf. Our aim is to provide our clients with the opportunity to play quality golf courses, obtain professional tuition, have fun and pleasure - all at affordable prices. We will also provide "off-the-course" entertainment for all of our clients, their families and guests while under contract with Lymac.

Courses

Lymac Golf and Leisure Promotion have acquired the reputation of being able to promote one of the largest selections of golf course availability to their clients. Over the last 15 years we have been able to achieve an unbeatable success rate in obtaining access to some of the most famous golfing links in a number of countries. Lymac concentrates its promotional activities at "the home of golf" - Scotland, but can also facilitate requests for other courses in the United Kingdom and indeed the remainder of Europe. As yet, we have not moved into the full international golfing arena, but plans are well ahead to enter into the United States of America in the next 2 years.

Leave the arrangements to us - we have the drive to book the course of your choice.

Equipment

Don't let the lack of equipment or difficulty of travel stand in your way - Lymac offer a full range of equipment-hire from a basic half-set of irons to tournament-grade clubs, bags, balls, trolleys and even electric "buggies" in your package. All the major suppliers of golf equipment are on contract with Lymac and we will guarantee to supply the equipment of your choice on request. We aim to please every golfer who registers with our firm and aim to make the choice of outing a time to remember.

If you want to be on par with the professionals - contact Lymac.

CHAIRMAN'S STATEMENT

INTRODUCTION

Last year has seen a remarkable growth in our business to the extent that we have increased our sales force by 5 per cent to cope with the increased demand for our product. In recent years the demand for vacations has increased - customers are now taking short breaks as well as the traditional summer vacations. Our Management Team has improved the service to the customers by offering a wide and varied selection of reasonably priced holidays and the customer has responded by demanding better accommodation, better meals and improved travel arrangements. All of these have been taken on board by the Management Team and this has resulted in an increase in sales in what must be considered to be "an expanding market".

RESULTS

I am pleased to report to our stockholders that earnings per share have increased by 28 per cent. This has enabled us to declare a final dividend of 3.55 pence, giving an overall increase for the year of 10.5 per cent. This increase is the highest for a number of years and it indicates the confidence which exists within our Company. We are determined to increase the efficiency of our activities within the Company over the next 3 years. Our Management Team is strong with many new proposals coming forward for a maintenance of our market position. We aim to target Short Breaks next year with the emphasis being on an improved option choice within Scotland. We also aim to improve the selection of European locations for both short and long stay holidays.

I am confident that we can exploit the growth opportunities which these offer.

BOARD

Two new Directors have been appointed recently. Mrs Hilary Whyte has extensive knowledge of European holidays and Mr John Black brings extensive experience and knowledge of the home market.

Mrs Marion Duncan and Mr James Clive retired from the Board and we wish them well in their retirement.

CHAIRMAN'S STATEMENT

> ASSIGNMENT 34
> Recall ASS14 and make the alterations indicated.
> Text to be displayed in 3 columns, each column to be 40 mm wide with 15 mm between.
> Left and right margins - 30 mm.
> Main heading to be on one line 55 mm from top edge of paper.
> INTRODUCTION, BOARD and STAFF to be in alignment 70 mm from top edge of paper.
> Retain type specifications as in Assignment 14.
> Print one copy. Save as ASS34.

INTRODUCTION

I am pleased to announce pre-tax profits for the year of £696 million. This is an increase of 6% on last year's figures. The post-tax figures for the current year have also shown a slight increase (1.5%) to £294 million which has covered the proposed dividend allowance for shareholders. As you will no doubt be aware the current market conditions, although slow, have improved and the prospects for next year appear to be brighter than first anticipated for our financial institution. Indeed, I would suggest that our organisation is in a much stronger position than many of our foreign competitors. This must be encouraging news for our shareholders and our customers alike.

Customers remain to be our top priority and this is reflected in the proposals and recommendations for the future as laid out in the Annual Report and Accounts.

BOARD

Since last year's report the Board have seen a number of changes. Two new members have been welcomed to the Board. Mr Kenneth McDonald joined us in November of last year as Senior Executive and Miss Eileen Fraser was appointed in February as Financial Controller (Foreign Investment). Mr Johnston Forsyth will be retiring at the forthcoming Annual General Meeting. Mr Forsyth joined the Board in 1976 and was Vice Chairman from 1981 to 1987. He has made a significant contribution to the organisation over many years, for which we, the Board are extremely grateful. I take this opportunity of wishing him a healthy and happy retirement.

STAFF

Our Management Staff have had a difficult year with the introduction of new management techniques. They have had to participate in many new aspects of organisational procedures and evaluation exercises over the last financial year. I am sure these new initiatives will be welcomed by staff at all levels in the very near future. On behalf of the Board I thank them for their continued effort and support.

> ASSIGNMENT 35
> Recall ASS15 and make the alterations indicated.
> Text to be displayed in 3 columns, each column to be 45 mm wide with 10 mm between.
> Left margin - 30 mm; right margin - 25 mm.
> Main heading to be on one line 60 mm from top edge of paper.
> <u>Living Area</u>, <u>Kitchen Area</u> and <u>Bathroom Area</u> to be in alignment 80 mm from top edge of paper.
> Retain type specifications as in Assignment 15.
> Print one copy. Save as ASS35.

HOME IMPROVEMENTS

Living Area

Great scope exists for the householder to improve the decor within the living areas of the home. Wall papering, painting, wood cladding, plastering and door replacement are all areas where the homeowner can make considerable savings both in time and money. Suppliers are only too willing to offer suggestions both in the method of construction and in the design of the living areas. This not only reassures the individual but also can save time and extra expense.

The quality of self-assembly furniture has given even wider scope for the individual and a wide range of furniture can be purchased and assembled using only the minimum of tools. In all self-assembly packs, the instructions are clear and concise.

Kitchen Area

Although many householders will engage professional help when installing a new kitchen, it is nevertheless possible to design and purchase units for the kitchen area from the DIY store. Considerable time and care should be taken, however, when measuring for wall units and cupboards. Problems can arise when wall measurements do not correspond to the unit sizes. Here again, however, the DIY enthusiast can undertake such a project knowing that expert advice and hints are readily available from the supplier.

Improving the kitchen is probably the most value-adding improvement which can be made within the home. Considering the amount of time spent in this area, it will also be one of the first areas of the home to be upgraded. Built-in or freestanding appliances can be costly additions to the kitchen but the majority of homes will have such appliances as the washing machine, tumble dryer, dishwasher, fridge or freezer and a microwave oven.

Bathroom Area

A replacement bathroom will be determined by not only your current needs, but also the likely future requirements for the area. Modern bathroom equipment is available from the DIY store in a wide choice of styles, shapes and colours. Planning the bathroom is critical since this can often be the smallest area in the home. Will the size and shape of the room allow for the installation of both a bath and a separate shower?

GOLF - "THE LYMAC WAY"

General Information

With the increasing amount of leisure time that is given to the general business community, it is important that this additional time is spent in a wise, healthy and enjoyable way. There's no better way to utilise this time than to participate in the art of "The Royal and Ancient Game". Lymac Golf and Leisure Promotion can offer a wide variety of options that will cater for all ages, male or female in the world of golf. Our aim is to provide our clients with the opportunity to play quality golf courses, obtain professional tuition, have fun and pleasure - all at affordable prices. We will also provide "off-the-course" entertainment for all of our clients, their families and guests while under contract with Lymac.

Courses

Lymac Golf and Leisure Promotion have acquired the reputation of being able to promote one of the largest selections of golf course availability to their clients. Over the last 15 years we have been able to achieve an unbeatable success rate in obtaining access to some of the most famous golfing links in a number of countries. Lymac concentrates its promotional activities at "the home of golf" - Scotland, but can also facilitate requests for other courses in the United Kingdom and indeed the remainder of Europe. As yet, we have not moved into the full international golfing arena, but plans are well ahead to enter into the United States of America in the next 2 years.

Leave the arrangements to us - we have the drive to book the course of your choice.

Equipment

Don't let the lack of equipment or difficulty of travel stand in your way - Lymac offer a full range of equipment-hire from a basic half-set of irons to tournament-grade clubs, bags, balls, trolleys and even electric "buggies" in your package. All the major suppliers of golf equipment are on contract with Lymac and we will guarantee to supply the equipment of your choice on request. We aim to please every golfer who registers with our firm and aim to make the choice of outing a time to remember.

If you want to be on par with the professionals - contact Lymac.

A & D TOURS PLC - Chairman's Statement

CHAIRMAN'S STATEMENT

INTRODUCTION

Last year has seen a remarkable growth in our business to the extent that we have increased our sales force by 5 per cent to cope with the increased demand for our product. In recent years the demand for vacations has increased - customers are now taking short breaks as well as the traditional summer vacations. Our Management Team has improved the service to the customers by offering a wide and varied selection of reasonably priced holidays and the customer has responded by demanding better accommodation, better meals and improved travel arrangements. All of these have been taken on board by the Management Team and this has resulted in an increase in sales in what must be considered to be "an expanding market".

RESULTS

I am pleased to report to our stockholders that earnings per share have increased by 28 per cent. This has enabled us to declare a final dividend of 3.55 pence, giving an overall increase for the year of 10.5 per cent. This increase is the highest for a number of years and it indicates the confidence which exists within our Company. We are determined to increase the efficiency of our activities within the Company over the next 3 years. Our Management Team is strong with many new proposals coming forward for a maintenance of our market position. We aim to target Short Breaks next year with the emphasis being on an improved option choice within Scotland. We also aim to improve the selection of European locations for both short and long stay holidays.

I am confident that we can exploit the growth opportunities which these offer.

BOARD

Two new Directors have been appointed recently. Mrs Hilary Whyte has extensive knowledge of European holidays and Mr John Black brings extensive experience and knowledge of the home market.

Mrs Marion Duncan and Mr James Clive retired from the Board and we wish them well in their retirement.

ALDON FINANCIAL SERVICES PLC - Chairman's Statement

CHAIRMAN'S STATEMENT

> **ASSIGNMENT 38**
> Recall ASS34 and make the alterations indicated.
> Add a header as shown (embolden) 10 mm from top edge of paper (Palatino 12 point).
> Horizontal lines (1 point) to begin and end in alignment with text.
> Vertical space between lines to be 13 mm.
> Main heading to commence 45 mm from top edge of paper.
> Print one copy. Save as ASS38.

INTRODUCTION

I am pleased to announce pre-tax profits for the year of £696 million. This is an increase of 6% on last year's figures. The post-tax figures for the current year have also shown a slight increase (1.5%) to £294 million which has covered the proposed dividend allowance for shareholders. As you will no doubt be aware the current market conditions, although slow, have improved and the prospects for next year appear to be brighter than first anticipated for our financial institution. Indeed, I would suggest that our organisation is in a much stronger position than many of our foreign competitors. This must be encouraging news for our shareholders and our customers alike.

Customers remain to be our top priority and this is reflected in the proposals and recommendations for the future as laid out in the Annual Report and Accounts.

BOARD

Since last year's report the Board have seen a number of changes. Two new members have been welcomed to the Board. Mr Kenneth McDonald joined us in November of last year as Senior Executive and Miss Eileen Fraser was appointed in February as Financial Controller (Foreign Investment). Mr Johnston Forsyth will be retiring at the forthcoming Annual General Meeting. Mr Forsyth joined the Board in 1976 and was Vice Chairman from 1981 to 1987. He has made a significant contribution to the organisation over many years, for which we, the Board are extremely grateful. I take this opportunity of wishing him a healthy and happy retirement.

STAFF

Our Management Staff have had a difficult year with the introduction of new management techniques. They have had to participate in many new aspects of organisational procedures and evaluation exercises over the last financial year. I am sure these new initiatives will be welcomed by staff at all levels in the very near future. On behalf of the Board I thank them for their continued effort and support.

DDA STORES PLC - The Impact of DO IT YOURSELF

HOME IMPROVEMENTS

> ASSIGNMENT 39
> Recall ASS35 and make the alterations indicated.
> Add a header as shown (in italics) 10 mm from top edge of paper (AvantGarde 12 point).
> Horizontal lines (0.5 point) to begin and end in alignment with text.
> Vertical space between lines to be 15 mm.
> Main heading to commence 50 mm from top edge of paper.
> Print one copy. Save as ASS39.

Living Area

Great scope exists for the householder to improve the decor within the living areas of the home. Wall papering, painting, wood cladding, plastering and door replacement are all areas where the homeowner can make considerable savings both in time and money. Suppliers are only too willing to offer suggestions both in the method of construction and in the design of the living areas. This not only reassures the individual but also can save time and extra expense.

The quality of self-assembly furniture has given even wider scope for the individual and a wide range of furniture can be purchased and assembled using only the minimum of tools. In all self-assembly packs, the instructions are clear and concise.

Kitchen Area

Although many householders will engage professional help when installing a new kitchen, it is nevertheless possible to design and purchase units for the kitchen area from the DIY store. Considerable time and care should be taken, however, when measuring for wall units and cupboards. Problems can arise when wall measurements do not correspond to the unit sizes. Here again, however, the DIY enthusiast can undertake such a project knowing that expert advice and hints are readily available from the supplier.

Improving the kitchen is probably the most value-adding improvement which can be made within the home. Considering the amount of time spent in this area, it will also be one of the first areas of the home to be upgraded. Built-in or freestanding appliances can be costly additions to the kitchen but the majority of homes will have such appliances as the washing machine, tumble dryer, dishwasher, fridge or freezer and a microwave oven.

Bathroom Area

A replacement bathroom will be determined by not only your current needs, but also the likely future requirements for the area. Modern bathroom equipment is available from the DIY store in a wide choice of styles, shapes and colours. Planning the bathroom is critical since this can often be the smallest area in the home. Will the size and shape of the room allow for the installation of both a bath and a separate shower?

LYMAC Golf and Leisure Promotion

GOLF - "THE LYMAC WAY"

> ASSIGNMENT 40
> Recall ASS36 and make the alterations indicated.
> Add a header as shown (embolden) 10 mm from top edge of paper (Palatino 12 point).
> Horizontal lines (1 point) to begin and end in alignment with text.
> Vertical space between lines to be 13 mm.
> Main heading to commence 45 mm from top edge of paper.
> Print one copy. Save as ASS40.

General Information

With the increasing amount of leisure time that is given to the general business community, it is important that this additional time is spent in a wise, healthy and enjoyable way. There's no better way to utilise this time than to participate in the art of "The Royal and Ancient Game". Lymac Golf and Leisure Promotion can offer a wide variety of options that will cater for all ages, male or female in the world of golf. Our aim is to provide our clients with the opportunity to play quality golf courses, obtain professional tuition, have fun and pleasure - all at affordable prices. We will also provide "off-the-course" entertainment for all of our clients, their families and guests while under contract with Lymac.

Courses

Lymac Golf and Leisure Promotion have acquired the reputation of being able to promote one of the largest selections of golf course availability to their clients. Over the last 15 years we have been able to achieve an unbeatable success rate in obtaining access to some of the most famous golfing links in a number of countries. Lymac concentrates its promotional activities at "the home of golf" - Scotland, but can also facilitate requests for other courses in the United Kingdom and indeed the remainder of Europe. As yet, we have not moved into the full international golfing arena, but plans are well ahead to enter into the United States of America in the next 2 years.

Leave the arrangements to us - we have the drive to book the course of your choice.

Equipment

Don't let the lack of equipment or difficulty of travel stand in your way - Lymac offer a full range of equipment-hire from a basic half-set of irons to tournament-grade clubs, bags, balls, trolleys and even electric "buggies" in your package. All the major suppliers of golf equipment are on contract with Lymac and we will guarantee to supply the equipment of your choice on request. We aim to please every golfer who registers with our firm and aim to make the choice of outing a time to remember.

If you want to be on par with the professionals - contact Lymac.

A & D TOURS PLC - *Chairman's Statement*

CHAIRMAN'S STATEMENT

> ASSIGNMENT 41
> Recall ASS37 and make the alterations indicated.
> Add a footer as shown (in italics) 20 mm from bottom edge of paper.
> Position the page number - 14 - at the left margin (AvantGarde 12 point).
> Horizontal lines (0.5 point) to begin and end in alignment with text.
> Vertical space between lines to be 15 mm.
> Print one copy. Save as ASS41.

INTRODUCTION

Last year has seen a remarkable growth in our business to the extent that we have increased our sales force by 5 per cent to cope with the increased demand for our product. In recent years the demand for vacations has increased - customers are now taking short breaks as well as the traditional summer vacations. Our Management Team has improved the service to the customers by offering a wide and varied selection of reasonably priced holidays and the customer has responded by demanding better accommodation, better meals and improved travel arrangements. All of these have been taken on board by the Management Team and this has resulted in an increase in sales in what must be considered to be "an expanding market".

RESULTS

I am pleased to report to our stockholders that earnings per share have increased by 28 per cent. This has enabled us to declare a final dividend of 3.55 pence, giving an overall increase for the year of 10.5 per cent. This increase is the highest for a number of years and it indicates the confidence which exists within our Company. We are determined to increase the efficiency of our activities within the Company over the next 3 years. Our Management Team is strong with many new proposals coming forward for a maintenance of our market position. We aim to target Short Breaks next year with the emphasis being on an improved option choice within Scotland. We also aim to improve the selection of European locations for both short and long stay holidays.

I am confident that we can exploit the growth opportunities which these offer.

BOARD

Two new Directors have been appointed recently. Mrs Hilary Whyte has extensive knowledge of European holidays and Mr John Black brings extensive experience and knowledge of the home market.

Mrs Marion Duncan and Mr James Clive retired from the Board and we wish them well in their retirement.

ALDON FINANCIAL SERVICES PLC - Chairman's Statement

CHAIRMAN'S STATEMENT

> ASSIGNMENT 42
> Recall ASS38 and make the alterations indicated.
> Add a footer as shown (embolden) 10 mm from bottom edge of paper.
> Position the footer - Page 37 - at the right margin (Palatino 12 point).
> Horizontal lines (1 point) to begin and end in alignment with text.
> Vertical space between lines to be 13 mm.
> Print one copy. Save as ASS42.

INTRODUCTION

I am pleased to announce pre-tax profits for the year of £696 million. This is an increase of 6% on last year's figures. The post-tax figures for the current year have also shown a slight increase (1.5%) to £294 million which has covered the proposed dividend allowance for shareholders. As you will no doubt be aware the current market conditions, although slow, have improved and the prospects for next year appear to be brighter than first anticipated for our financial institution. Indeed, I would suggest that our organisation is in a much stronger position than many of our foreign competitors. This must be encouraging news for our shareholders and our customers alike.

Customers remain to be our top priority and this is reflected in the proposals and recommendations for the future as laid out in the Annual Report and Accounts.

BOARD

Since last year's report the Board have seen a number of changes. Two new members have been welcomed to the Board. Mr Kenneth McDonald joined us in November of last year as Senior Executive and Miss Eileen Fraser was appointed in February as Financial Controller (Foreign Investment). Mr Johnston Forsyth will be retiring at the forthcoming Annual General Meeting. Mr Forsyth joined the Board in 1976 and was Vice Chairman from 1981 to 1987. He has made a significant contribution to the organisation over many years, for which we, the Board are extremely grateful. I take this opportunity of wishing him a healthy and happy retirement.

STAFF

Our Management Staff have had a difficult year with the introduction of new management techniques. They have had to participate in many new aspects of organisational procedures and evaluation exercises over the last financial year. I am sure these new initiatives will be welcomed by staff at all levels in the very near future. On behalf of the Board I thank them for their continued effort and support.

DDA STORES PLC - The Impact of DO IT YOURSELF

HOME IMPROVEMENTS

> ASSIGNMENT 43
> Recall ASS39 and make the alterations indicated.
> Add a footer as shown (in italics) 20 mm from bottom edge of paper.
> Position the page number - 6 - at the left margin (AvantGarde 12 point).
> Horizontal lines (0.5 point) to begin and end in alignment with text.
> Vertical space between lines to be 15 mm.
> Print one copy. Save as ASS43.

Living Area

Great scope exists for the householder to improve the decor within the living areas of the home. Wall papering, painting, wood cladding, plastering and door replacement are all areas where the homeowner can make considerable savings both in time and money. Suppliers are only too willing to offer suggestions both in the method of construction and in the design of the living areas. This not only reassures the individual but also can save time and extra expense.

The quality of self-assembly furniture has given even wider scope for the individual and a wide range of furniture can be purchased and assembled using only the minimum of tools. In all self-assembly packs, the instructions are clear and concise.

Kitchen Area

Although many householders will engage professional help when installing a new kitchen, it is nevertheless possible to design and purchase units for the kitchen area from the DIY store. Considerable time and care should be taken, however, when measuring for wall units and cupboards. Problems can arise when wall measurements do not correspond to the unit sizes. Here again, however, the DIY enthusiast can undertake such a project knowing that expert advice and hints are readily available from the supplier.

Improving the kitchen is probably the most value-adding improvement which can be made within the home. Considering the amount of time spent in this area, it will also be one of the first areas of the home to be upgraded. Built-in or freestanding appliances can be costly additions to the kitchen but the majority of homes will have such appliances as the washing machine, tumble dryer, dishwasher, fridge or freezer and a microwave oven.

Bathroom Area

A replacement bathroom will be determined by not only your current needs, but also the likely future requirements for the area. Modern bathroom equipment is available from the DIY store in a wide choice of styles, shapes and colours. Planning the bathroom is critical since this can often be the smallest area in the home. Will the size and shape of the room allow for the installation of both a bath and a separate shower?

LYMAC Golf and Leisure Promotion

GOLF - "THE LYMAC WAY"

> ASSIGNMENT 44
> Recall ASS40 and make the alterations indicated.
> Add a footer as shown (embolden) 10 mm from bottom edge of paper.
> Position the footer - LGLP - at the left margin (Palatino 12 point).
> Horizontal lines (1 point) to begin and end in alignment with text.
> Vertical space between lines to be 13 mm.
> Print one copy. Save as ASS44.

General Information

With the increasing amount of leisure time that is given to the general business community, it is important that this additional time is spent in a wise, healthy and enjoyable way. There's no better way to utilise this time than to participate in the art of "The Royal and Ancient Game". Lymac Golf and Leisure Promotion can offer a wide variety of options that will cater for all ages, male or female in the world of golf. Our aim is to provide our clients with the opportunity to play quality golf courses, obtain professional tuition, have fun and pleasure - all at affordable prices. We will also provide "off-the-course" entertainment for all of our clients, their families and guests while under contract with Lymac.

Courses

Lymac Golf and Leisure Promotion have acquired the reputation of being able to promote one of the largest selections of golf course availability to their clients. Over the last 15 years we have been able to achieve an unbeatable success rate in obtaining access to some of the most famous golfing links in a number of countries. Lymac concentrates its promotional activities at "the home of golf" - Scotland, but can also facilitate requests for other courses in the United Kingdom and indeed the remainder of Europe. As yet, we have not moved into the full international golfing arena, but plans are well ahead to enter into the United States of America in the next 2 years.

Leave the arrangements to us - we have the drive to book the course of your choice.

Equipment

Don't let the lack of equipment or difficulty of travel stand in your way - Lymac offer a full range of equipment-hire from a basic half-set of irons to tournament-grade clubs, bags, balls, trolleys and even electric "buggies" in your package. All the major suppliers of golf equipment are on contract with Lymac and we will guarantee to supply the equipment of your choice on request. We aim to please every golfer who registers with our firm and aim to make the choice of outing a time to remember.

If you want to be on par with the professionals - contact Lymac.

LGLP

A & D TOURS PLC - Chairman's Statement

CHAIRMAN'S STATEMENT

> **ASSIGNMENT 45**
> Recall ASS41 and make the alterations indicated.
> Centre the header text and the footer text.
> Centre the main heading.
> Print one copy. Save as ASS45.

INTRODUCTION

Last year has seen a remarkable growth in our business to the extent that we have increased our sales force by 5 per cent to cope with the increased demand for our product. In recent years the demand for vacations has increased - customers are now taking short breaks as well as the traditional summer vacations. Our Management Team has improved the service to the customers by offering a wide and varied selection of reasonably priced holidays and the customer has responded by demanding better accommodation, better meals and improved travel arrangements. All of these have been taken on board by the Management Team and this has resulted in an increase in sales in what must be considered to be "an expanding market".

RESULTS

I am pleased to report to our stockholders that earnings per share have increased by 28 per cent. This has enabled us to declare a final dividend of 3.55 pence, giving an overall increase for the year of 10.5 per cent. This increase is the highest for a number of years and it indicates the confidence which exists within our Company. We are determined to increase the efficiency of our activities within the Company over the next 3 years. Our Management Team is strong with many new proposals coming forward for a maintenance of our market position. We aim to target Short Breaks next year with the emphasis being on an improved option choice within Scotland. We also aim to improve the selection of European locations for both short and long stay holidays.

I am confident that we can exploit the growth opportunities which these offer.

BOARD

Two new Directors have been appointed recently. Mrs Hilary Whyte has extensive knowledge of European holidays and Mr John Black brings extensive experience and knowledge of the home market.

Mrs Marion Duncan and Mr James Clive retired from the Board and we wish them well in their retirement.

14

ALDON FINANCIAL SERVICES PLC - Chairman's Statement

CHAIRMAN'S STATEMENT

> ASSIGNMENT 46
> Recall ASS42 and make the alterations indicated.
> Centre the header text and the footer text.
> Centre the main heading.
> Print one copy. Save as ASS46.

INTRODUCTION

I am pleased to announce pre-tax profits for the year of £696 million. This is an increase of 6% on last year's figures. The post-tax figures for the current year have also shown a slight increase (1.5%) to £294 million which has covered the proposed dividend allowance for shareholders. As you will no doubt be aware the current market conditions, although slow, have improved and the prospects for next year appear to be brighter than first anticipated for our financial institution. Indeed, I would suggest that our organisation is in a much stronger position than many of our foreign competitors. This must be encouraging news for our shareholders and our customers alike.

Customers remain to be our top priority and this is reflected in the proposals and recommendations for the future as laid out in the Annual Report and Accounts.

BOARD

Since last year's report the Board have seen a number of changes. Two new members have been welcomed to the Board. Mr Kenneth McDonald joined us in November of last year as Senior Executive and Miss Eileen Fraser was appointed in February as Financial Controller (Foreign Investment). Mr Johnston Forsyth will be retiring at the forthcoming Annual General Meeting. Mr Forsyth joined the Board in 1976 and was Vice Chairman from 1981 to 1987. He has made a significant contribution to the organisation over many years, for which we, the Board are extremely grateful. I take this opportunity of wishing him a healthy and happy retirement.

STAFF

Our Management Staff have had a difficult year with the introduction of new management techniques. They have had to participate in many new aspects of organisational procedures and evaluation exercises over the last financial year. I am sure these new initiatives will be welcomed by staff at all levels in the very near future. On behalf of the Board I thank them for their continued effort and support.

HOME IMPROVEMENTS

> **ASSIGNMENT 47**
> Recall ASS43 and make the alterations indicated.
> Centre the header text and the footer text.
> Centre the main heading.
> Print one copy. Save as ASS47.

Living Area

Great scope exists for the householder to improve the decor within the living areas of the home. Wall papering, painting, wood cladding, plastering and door replacement are all areas where the homeowner can make considerable savings both in time and money. Suppliers are only too willing to offer suggestions both in the method of construction and in the design of the living areas. This not only reassures the individual but also can save time and extra expense.

The quality of self-assembly furniture has given even wider scope for the individual and a wide range of furniture can be purchased and assembled using only the minimum of tools. In all self-assembly packs, the instructions are clear and concise.

Kitchen Area

Although many householders will engage professional help when installing a new kitchen, it is nevertheless possible to design and purchase units for the kitchen area from the DIY store. Considerable time and care should be taken, however, when measuring for wall units and cupboards. Problems can arise when wall measurements do not correspond to the unit sizes. Here again, however, the DIY enthusiast can undertake such a project knowing that expert advice and hints are readily available from the supplier.

Improving the kitchen is probably the most value-adding improvement which can be made within the home. Considering the amount of time spent in this area, it will also be one of the first areas of the home to be upgraded. Built-in or freestanding appliances can be costly additions to the kitchen but the majority of homes will have such appliances as the washing machine, tumble dryer, dishwasher, fridge or freezer and a microwave oven.

Bathroom Area

A replacement bathroom will be determined by not only your current needs, but also the likely future requirements for the area. Modern bathroom equipment is available from the DIY store in a wide choice of styles, shapes and colours. Planning the bathroom is critical since this can often be the smallest area in the home. Will the size and shape of the room allow for the installation of both a bath and a separate shower?

LYMAC Golf and Leisure Promotion

GOLF - "THE LYMAC WAY"

> **ASSIGNMENT 48**
> Recall ASS44 and make the alterations indicated.
> Centre the header text and the footer text.
> Centre the main heading.
> Print one copy. Save as ASS48.

General Information

With the increasing amount of leisure time that is given to the general business community, it is important that this additional time is spent in a wise, healthy and enjoyable way. There's no better way to utilise this time than to participate in the art of "The Royal and Ancient Game". Lymac Golf and Leisure Promotion can offer a wide variety of options that will cater for all ages, male or female in the world of golf. Our aim is to provide our clients with the opportunity to play quality golf courses, obtain professional tuition, have fun and pleasure - all at affordable prices. We will also provide "off-the-course" entertainment for all of our clients, their families and guests while under contract with Lymac.

Courses

Lymac Golf and Leisure Promotion have acquired the reputation of being able to promote one of the largest selections of golf course availability to their clients. Over the last 15 years we have been able to achieve an unbeatable success rate in obtaining access to some of the most famous golfing links in a number of countries. Lymac concentrates its promotional activities at "the home of golf" - Scotland, but can also facilitate requests for other courses in the United Kingdom and indeed the remainder of Europe. As yet, we have not moved into the full international golfing arena, but plans are well ahead to enter into the United States of America in the next 2 years.

Leave the arrangements to us - we have the drive to book the course of your choice.

Equipment

Don't let the lack of equipment or difficulty of travel stand in your way - Lymac offer a full range of equipment-hire from a basic half-set of irons to tournament-grade clubs, bags, balls, trolleys and even electric "buggies" in your package. All the major suppliers of golf equipment are on contract with Lymac and we will guarantee to supply the equipment of your choice on request. We aim to please every golfer who registers with our firm and aim to make the choice of outing a time to remember.

If you want to be on par with the professionals - contact Lymac.

LGLP

A & D TOURS PLC - Chairman's Statement

CHAIRMAN'S STATEMENT

INTRODUCTION

Last year has seen a remarkable growth in our business to the extent that we have increased our sales force by 5 per cent to cope with the increased demand for our product. In recent years the demand for vacations has increased - customers are now taking short breaks as well as the traditional summer vacations. Our Management Team has improved the service to the customers by offering a wide and varied selection of reasonably priced holidays and the customer has responded by demanding better accommodation, better meals and improved travel arrangements. All of these have been taken on board by the Management Team and this has resulted in an increase in sales in what must be considered to be "an expanding market".

RESULTS

I am pleased to report to our stockholders that earnings per share have increased by 28 per cent. This has enabled us to declare a final dividend of 3.55 pence, giving an overall increase for the year of 10.5 per cent. This increase is the highest for a number of years and it indicates the confidence which exists within our Company. We are determined to increase the efficiency of our activities within the Company over the next 3 years. Our Management Team is strong with many new proposals coming forward for a maintenance of our market position. We aim to target Short Breaks next year with the emphasis being on an improved option choice within Scotland. We also aim to improve the selection of European locations for both short and long stay holidays.

I am confident that we can exploit the growth opportunities which these offer.

BOARD

Two new Directors have been appointed recently. Mrs Hilary Whyte has extensive knowledge of European holidays and Mr John Black brings extensive experience and knowledge of the home market.

Mrs Marion Duncan and Mr James Clive retired from the Board and we wish them well in their retirement.

ASSIGNMENT 49
Recall ASS45 and make the alterations indicated.
Insert box 40 x 60 mm (0.5 point) to commence at 115 mm from left edge and 120 mm from top edge of paper.
Text should wrap around box as indicated.
Paragraph text to be in AvantGarde 9 point.
Print one copy. Save as ASS49.

ALDON FINANCIAL SERVICES PLC - Chairman's Statement

CHAIRMAN'S STATEMENT

INTRODUCTION

I am pleased to announce pre-tax profits for the year of £696 million. This is an increase of 6% on last year's figures. The post-tax figures for the current year have also shown a slight increase (1.5%) to £294 million which has covered the proposed dividend allowance for shareholders. As you will no doubt be aware the current market conditions, although slow, have improved and the prospects for next year appear to be brighter than first anticipated for our financial institution. Indeed, I would suggest that our organisation is in a much stronger position than many of our foreign competitors. This must be encouraging news for our shareholders and our customers alike.

Customers remain to be our top priority and this is reflected in the proposals and recommendations for the future as laid out in the Annual Report and Accounts.

BOARD

Since last year's report the Board have seen a number of changes. Two new members have been welcomed to the Board. Mr Kenneth McDonald joined us in November of last year as Senior Executive and Miss Eileen Fraser was appointed in February as Financial Controller (Foreign Investment). Mr Johnston Forsyth will be retiring at the forthcoming Annual General Meeting. Mr Forsyth joined the Board in 1976 and was Vice Chairman from 1981 to 1987. He has made a significant contribution to the organisation over many years, for which we, the Board are extremely grateful. I take this opportunity of wishing him a healthy and happy retirement.

STAFF

Our Management Staff have had a difficult year with the introduction of new management techniques. They have had to participate in many new aspects of organisational procedures and evaluation exercises over the last financial year. I am sure these new initiatives will be welcomed by staff at all levels in the very near future. On behalf of the Board I thank them for their continued effort and support.

ASSIGNMENT 50
Recall ASS46 and make the alterations indicated.
Insert box 45 x 60 mm (1 point) to commence at 55 mm from left edge and 100 mm from top edge of paper. Text should wrap around box as indicated. Paragraph text to be in Palatino 9 point. Print one copy. Save as ASS50.

DDA STORES PLC - The Impact of DO IT YOURSELF

HOME IMPROVEMENTS

Living Area

Great scope exists for the householder to improve the decor within the living areas of the home. Wall papering, painting, wood cladding, plastering and door replacement are all areas where the homeowner can make considerable savings both in time and money. Suppliers are only too willing to offer suggestions both in the method of construction and in the design of the living areas. This not only reassures the individual but also can save time and extra expense.

The quality of self-assembly furniture has given even wider scope for the individual and a wide range of furniture can be purchased and assembled using only the minimum of tools. In all self-assembly packs, the instructions are clear and concise.

Kitchen Area

Although many householders will engage professional help when installing a new kitchen, it is nevertheless possible to design and purchase units for the kitchen area from the DIY store. Considerable time and care should be taken, however, when measuring for wall units and cupboards. Problems can arise when wall measurements do not correspond to the unit sizes. Here again, however, the DIY enthusiast can undertake such a project knowing that expert advice and hints are readily available from the supplier.

Improving the kitchen is probably the most value-adding improvement which can be made within the home. Considering the amount of time spent in this area, it will also be one of the first areas of the home to be upgraded. Built-in or freestanding appliances can be costly additions to the kitchen but the majority of homes will have such appliances as the washing machine, tumble dryer, dishwasher, fridge or freezer and a microwave oven.

Bathroom Area

A replacement bathroom will be determined by not only your current needs, but also the likely future requirements for the area. Modern bathroom equipment is available from the DIY store in a wide choice of styles, shapes and colours. Planning the bathroom is critical since this can often be the smallest area in the home. Will the size and shape of the room allow for the installation of both a bath and a separate shower?

ASSIGNMENT 51
Recall ASS47 and make the alterations indicated.
Insert box 40 x 60 mm (0.5 point) to commence at 115 mm from left edge and 120 mm from top edge of paper.
Text should wrap around box as indicated.
Paragraph text to be in AvantGarde 8 point.
Print one copy. Save as ASS51.

LYMAC Golf and Leisure Promotion

GOLF - "THE LYMAC WAY"

General Information

With the increasing amount of leisure time that is given to the general business community, it is important that this additional time is spent in a wise, healthy and enjoyable way. There's no better way to utilise this time than to participate in the art of "The Royal and Ancient Game". Lymac Golf and Leisure Promotion can offer a wide variety of options that will cater for all ages, male or female in the world of golf. Our aim is to provide our clients with the opportunity to play quality golf courses, obtain professional tuition, have fun and pleasure - all at affordable prices. We will also provide "off-the-course" entertainment for all of our clients, their families and guests while under contract with Lymac.

Courses

Lymac Golf and Leisure Promotion have acquired the reputation of being able to promote one of the largest selections of golf course availability to their clients. Over the last 15 years we have been able to achieve an unbeatable success rate in obtaining access to some of the most famous golfing links in a number of countries. Lymac concentrates its promotional activities at "the home of golf" - Scotland, but can also facilitate requests for other courses in the United Kingdom and indeed the remainder of Europe. As yet, we have not moved into the full international golfing arena, but plans are well ahead to enter into the United States of America in the next 2 years.

Leave the arrangements to us - we have the drive to book the course of your choice.

Equipment

Don't let the lack of equipment or difficulty of travel stand in your way - Lymac offer a full range of equipment-hire from a basic half-set of irons to tournament-grade clubs, bags, balls, trolleys and even electric "buggies" in your package. All the major suppliers of golf equipment are on contract with Lymac and we will guarantee to supply the equipment of your choice on request. We aim to please every golfer who registers with our firm and aim to make the choice of outing a time to remember.

If you want to be on par with the professionals - contact Lymac.

ASSIGNMENT 52
Recall ASS48 and make the alterations indicated.
Insert box 45 x 60 mm (1 point) to commence at 55 mm from left edge and 100 mm from top edge of paper.
Text should wrap around box as indicated.
Paragraph text to be in Palatino 9 point.
Print one copy. Save as ASS52.

LGLP

CHAIRMAN'S STATEMENT

> ASSIGNMENT 53
> Recall ASS9 and make the alterations indicated.
> Make a new paragraph at "Our Management Team . . ." in the RESULTS section.
> Text has been added after ". . . long stay holidays." in the RESULTS section.
> Text has been added after ". . . in their retirement." in the BOARD section.
> Paragraph text to be in Courier 12 point.
> Page number - 1 - to be 10 mm from bottom edge of paper at right margin.
> Page number - 2 - to be 10 mm from bottom edge of paper at left margin (Courier 12 point).
> Print one copy of both pages. Save as ASS53.

INTRODUCTION

Last year has seen a remarkable growth in our business to the extent that we have increased our sales force by 5 per cent to cope with the increased demand for our product. In recent years the demand for vacations has increased - customers are now taking short breaks as well as the traditional summer vacations. Our Management Team has improved the service to the customers by offering a wide and varied selection of reasonably priced holidays and the customer has responded by demanding better accommodation, better meals and improved travel arrangements. All of these have been taken on board by the Management Team and this has resulted in an increase in sales in what must be considered to be "an expanding market".

RESULTS

I am pleased to report to our stockholders that earnings per share have increased by 28 per cent. This has enabled us to declare a final dividend of 3.55 pence, giving an overall increase for the year of 10.5 per cent. This increase is the highest for a number of years and it indicates the confidence which exists within our Company. We are determined to increase the efficiency of our activities within the Company over the next 3 years.

Our Management Team is strong with many new proposals coming forward for a maintenance of our market position. We aim to target Short Breaks next year with the emphasis being on an improved option choice within Scotland. We also aim to improve the selection of European locations for both short and long stay holidays.

The Board has agreed that the Marketing section should be strengthened and that the principal focus will be on the areas mentioned above. We shall be making substantial investments in our Short Break hotel chain and we intend to improve the profitability of a number of our European hotels, particularly in Spain. We are also exploring and evaluating opportunities for profitable growth in Germany and Italy.

Economic conditions fluctuated considerably over the last 12 months and this had a direct influence on our results for the period. In spite of these conditions, I am pleased to report a satisfactory performance.

I am confident that we can exploit the growth opportunities which these offer.

BOARD

Two new Directors have been appointed recently. Mrs Hilary Whyte has extensive knowledge of European holidays and Mr John Black brings extensive experience and knowledge of the home market.

Mrs Marion Duncan and Mr James Clive retired from the Board and we wish them well in their retirement.

The names of the Directors of the Company are shown on page 29 of the Annual Report. Mr Peter Johnstone, Mrs Joan Brownlee and Dr Robert Fleming will retire by rotation at the Annual General Meeting and offer themselves for re-election.

Mrs Pauline Hogarth and Dr William Russell were appointed Directors last year and they will retire at the Annual General Meeting and offer themselves for election.

CHAIRMAN'S STATEMENT

> ASSIGNMENT 54
> Recall ASS10 and make the alterations indicated.
> Additional text (2 paragraphs) has been added to the INTRODUCTION section after ". . . as laid out in the Annual Report and Accounts."
> Make a new paragraph at "Mr Kenneth McDonald joined us in November . . ."
> Paragraph text to be in Pica 12 point.
> Page number - 1 - to be 15 mm from bottom edge of paper at right margin.
> Page number - 2 - to be 15 mm from bottom edge of paper at left margin (Pica 12 point).
> Print one copy of both pages. Save as ASS54.

INTRODUCTION

I am pleased to announce pre-tax profits for the year of £696 million. This is an increase of 6% on last year's figures. The post-tax figures for the current year have also shown a slight increase (1.5%) to £294 million which has covered the proposed dividend allowance for shareholders. As you will no doubt be aware the current market conditions, although slow, have improved and the prospects for next year appear to be brighter than first anticipated for our financial institution. Indeed, I would suggest that our organisation is in a much stronger position than many of our foreign competitors. This must be encouraging news for our shareholders and our customers alike.

Customers remain to be our top priority and this is reflected in the proposals and recommendations for the future as laid out in the Annual Report and Accounts.

Despite the previous financial year being difficult for most financial institutions, Aldon Financial Services PLC retained its share price and ended the year 9% above the FT All-Share Index (the third consecutive year that Aldon's Share Price has been above this index). Once again there was no call on shareholders (for the eighteenth consecutive year) and the dividend was increased by 11% on last year's figures. This development of progressive increases keeps our organisation in line with the objective stated in the Board's strategic plan "to produce shareholders' long-term, superior total returns, comprising continued dividend growth and appreciation in the share price".

In spite of both economic and competitive conditions the performance of our organisation retains our position in the Financial Services sector.

BOARD

Since last year's report the Board have seen a number of changes. Two new members have been welcomed to the Board.

Mr Kenneth McDonald joined us in November of last year as Senior Executive and Miss Eileen Fraser was appointed in February as Financial Controller (Foreign Investment). Mr Johnston Forsyth will be retiring at the forthcoming Annual General Meeting. Mr Forsyth joined the Board in 1976 and was Vice Chairman from 1981 to 1987. He has made a significant contribution to the organisation over many years, for which we, the Board are extremely grateful. I take this opportunity of wishing him a healthy and happy retirement.

STAFF

Our Management Staff have had a difficult year with the introduction of new management techniques. They have had to participate in many new aspects of organisational procedures and evaluation exercises over the last financial year. I am sure these new initiatives will be welcomed by staff at all levels in the very near future. On behalf of the Board I thank them for their continued effort and support.

HOME IMPROVEMENTS

> ASSIGNMENT 55
> Recall ASS11 and make the alterations indicated.
> Two paragraphs have been added after "... and a separate shower?" at the end of the passage.
> Paragraph text to be in Courier 10 point.
> Page number - 1 - to be 10 mm from bottom edge of paper at right margin.
> Page number - 2 - to be 10 mm from bottom edge of paper at left margin (Courier 12 point).
> Print one copy of both pages. Save as ASS55.

Living Area

Great scope exists for the householder to improve the decor within the living areas of the home. Wall papering, painting, wood cladding, plastering and door replacement are all areas where the homeowner can make considerable savings both in time and money. Suppliers are only too willing to offer suggestions both in the method of construction and in the design of the living areas. This not only reassures the individual but also can save time and extra expense.

The quality of self-assembly furniture has given even wider scope for the individual and a wide range of furniture can be purchased and assembled using only the minimum of tools. In all self-assembly packs, the instructions are clear and concise.

Kitchen Area

Although many householders will engage professional help when installing a new kitchen, it is nevertheless possible to design and purchase units for the kitchen area from the DIY store. Considerable time and care should be taken, however, when measuring for wall units and cupboards. Problems can arise when wall measurements do not correspond to the unit sizes. Here again, however, the DIY enthusiast can undertake such a project knowing that expert advice and hints are readily available from the supplier.

Improving the kitchen is probably the most value-adding improvement which can be made within the home. Considering the amount of time spent in this area, it will also be one of the first areas of the home to be upgraded. Built-in or freestanding appliances can be costly additions to the kitchen but the majority of homes will have such appliances as the washing machine, tumble dryer, dishwasher, fridge or freezer and a microwave oven.

Bathroom Area

A replacement bathroom will be determined by not only your current needs, but also the likely future requirements for the area. Modern bathroom equipment is available from the DIY store in a wide choice of styles, shapes and colours. Planning the bathroom is critical since this can often be the smallest area in the home. Will the size and shape of the room allow for the installation of both a bath and a separate shower?

Pedestal basins are available in various sizes and shapes and can be either wall mounted or can be fitted in a corner. The WC cistern can often be concealed behind the wall thus adding to the available space within the bathroom. Apart from these basic items, some consideration must be given to the lighting within the bathroom. If in doubt, call in the experts.

DIY has become popular in British households over the last decade. Fifteen years ago, the householder would call in the experts be they plumbers, plasterers, painters or joiners. Today it is not uncommon for both the man and the woman of the household to undertake tasks around the house. By offering a wide choice, competitive prices and convenient shopping hours, DIY stores have contributed greatly to the popularity of DO IT YOURSELF.

GOLF - "THE LYMAC WAY"

> ASSIGNMENT 56
> Recall ASS12 and make the alterations indicated.
> Additional text has been added to the Equipment section after "... choice on request."
> Paragraph text to be in Pica 12 point.
> Page number - 1 - to be 15 mm from bottom edge of paper at right margin.
> Page number - 2 - to be 15 mm from bottom edge of paper at left margin (Pica 12 point).
> Print one copy of both pages. Save as ASS56.

General Information

With the increasing amount of leisure time that is given to the general business community, it is important that this additional time is spent in a wise, healthy and enjoyable way. There's no better way to utilise this time than to participate in the art of "The Royal and Ancient Game". Lymac Golf and Leisure Promotion can offer a wide variety of options that will cater for all ages, male or female in the world of golf. Our aim is to provide our clients with the opportunity to play quality golf courses, obtain professional tuition, have fun and pleasure - all at affordable prices. We will also provide "off-the-course" entertainment for all of our clients, their families and guests while under contract with Lymac.

Courses

Lymac Golf and Leisure Promotion have acquired the reputation of being able to promote one of the largest selections of golf course availability to their clients. Over the last 15 years we have been able to achieve an unbeatable success rate in obtaining access to some of the most famous golfing links in a number of countries. Lymac concentrates its promotional activities at "the home of golf" - Scotland, but can also facilitate requests for other courses in the United Kingdom and indeed the remainder of Europe. As yet, we have not moved into the full international golfing arena, but plans are well ahead to enter into the United States of America in the next 2 years.

Leave the arrangements to us - we have the drive to book the course of your choice.

Equipment

Don't let the lack of equipment or difficulty of travel stand in your way - Lymac offer a full range of equipment-hire from a basic half-set of irons to tournament-grade clubs, bags, balls, trolleys and even electric "buggies" in your package. All the major suppliers of golf equipment are on contract with Lymac and we will guarantee to supply the equipment of your choice on request. As well as providing the hire of equipment, we will also supply each golfer with a Lymac Presentation Pack (free of charge). Each pack contains 6 golf balls, a golf glove, tees, markers and a club tie - all items have the Lymac logo. Should you require any additional items which have not been listed please contact our representative who will be happy to make the necessary arrangements to meet your requirements. We aim to please every golfer who registers with our firm and aim to make the choice of outing a time to remember.

If you want to be on par with the professionals - contact Lymac.

A & D TOURS PLC - Chairman's Statement

CHAIRMAN'S STATEMENT

INTRODUCTION

> ASSIGNMENT 57
> Instructions on following page.

Last year has seen a remarkable growth in our business to the extent that we have increased our sales force by 5 per cent to cope with the increased demand for our product. In recent years the demand for vacations has increased - customers are now taking short breaks as well as the traditional summer vacations. Our Management Team has improved the service to the customers by offering a wide and varied selection of reasonably priced holidays and the customer has responded by demanding better accommodation, better meals and improved travel arrangements. All of these have been taken on board by the Management Team and this has resulted in an increase in sales in what must be considered to be "an expanding market".

RESULTS

I am pleased to report to our stockholders that earnings per share have increased by 28 per cent. This has enabled us to declare a final dividend of 3.55 pence, giving an overall increase for the year of 10.5 per cent. This increase is the highest for a number of years and it indicates the confidence which exists within our Company. We are determined to increase the efficiency of our activities within the Company over the next 3 years.

Our Management Team is strong with many new proposals coming forward for a maintenance of our market position. We aim to target Short Breaks next year with the emphasis being on an improved option choice within Scotland. We also aim to improve the selection of European locations for both short and long stay holidays.

The Board has agreed that the Marketing section should be strengthened and that the principal focus will be on the areas mentioned above. We shall be making substantial investments in our Short Break hotel chain and we intend to improve the profitability of a number of our European hotels, particularly in Spain. We are also exploring and evaluating opportunities for profitable growth in Germany and Italy.

Economic conditions fluctuated considerably over the last 12 months and this had a direct influence on our results for the period. In spite of these conditions, I am pleased to report a satisfactory performance.

I am confident that we can exploit the growth opportunities which these offer.

BOARD

Two new Directors have been appointed recently. Mrs Hilary Whyte has extensive knowledge of European holidays and Mr John Black brings extensive experience and knowledge of the home market.

Mrs Marion Duncan and Mr James Clive retired from the Board and we wish them well in their retirement.

The names of the Directors of the Company are shown on page 29 of the Annual Report. Mr Peter Johnstone, Mrs Joan Brownlee and Dr Robert Fleming will retire by rotation at the Annual General Meeting and offer themselves for re-election.

Mrs Pauline Hogarth and Dr William Russell were appointed Directors last year and they will retire at the Annual General Meeting and offer themselves for election.

ASSIGNMENT 57
Recall ASS53 and make the alterations indicated.
Text to be arranged in 2 columns - 70 mm wide; 15 mm space between.
Page 1 - 30 mm left margin; 25 mm right margin; 25 mm bottom margin.
Page 2 - 25 mm left margin; 30 mm right margin; top margin 25 mm.
Type specifications - AvantGarde 14 point.
Add a header (embolden) on page 1 as shown 10 mm from top edge of paper (AvantGarde 16 point).
Horizontal lines (0.5 point) to begin and end in alignment with text.
Vertical space between lines to be 20 mm.
Main heading - **CHAIRMAN'S STATEMENT** - to commence 40 mm from top edge of paper.
INTRODUCTION to commence 50 mm from top edge of paper.
Centre page numbers 15 mm from bottom edge of paper.
Print one copy of both pages. Save as ASS57.

ALDON FINANCIAL SERVICES PLC - Chairman's Statement

CHAIRMAN'S STATEMENT

> ASSIGNMENT 58
> Instructions on following page.

INTRODUCTION

I am pleased to announce pre-tax profits for the year of £696 million. This is an increase of 6% on last year's figures. The post-tax figures for the current year have also shown a slight increase (1.5%) to £294 million which has covered the proposed dividend allowance for shareholders. As you will no doubt be aware the current market conditions, although slow, have improved and the prospects for next year appear to be brighter than first anticipated for our financial institution. Indeed, I would suggest that our organisation is in a much stronger position than many of our foreign competitors. This must be encouraging news for our shareholders and our customers alike.

Customers remain to be our top priority and this is reflected in the proposals and recommendations for the future as laid out in the Annual Report and Accounts.

Despite the previous financial year being difficult for most financial institutions, Aldon Financial Services PLC retained its share price and ended the year 9% above the FT All-Share Index (the third consecutive year that Aldon's Share Price has been above this index). Once again there was no call on shareholders (for the eighteenth consecutive year) and the dividend was increased by 11% on last year's figures. This development of progressive increases keeps our organisation in line with the objective stated in the Board's strategic plan "to produce shareholders' long-term, superior total returns, comprising continued dividend growth and appreciation in the share price".

In spite of both economic and competitive conditions the performance of our organisation retains our position in the Financial Services sector.

BOARD

Since last year's report the Board have seen a number of changes. Two new members have been welcomed to the Board.

Mr Kenneth McDonald joined us in November of last year as Senior Executive and Miss Eileen Fraser was appointed in February as Financial Controller (Foreign Investment). Mr Johnston Forsyth will be retiring at the forthcoming Annual General Meeting. Mr Forsyth joined the Board in 1976 and was Vice Chairman from 1981 to 1987. He has made a significant contribution to the organisation over many years, for which we, the Board are extremely grateful. I take this opportunity of wishing him a healthy and happy retirement.

STAFF

Our Management Staff have had a difficult year with the introduction of new management techniques. They have had to participate in many new aspects of organisational procedures and evaluation exercises over the last financial year. I am sure these new initiatives will be welcomed by staff at all levels in the very near future. On behalf of the Board I thank them for their continued effort and support.

ASSIGNMENT 58
Recall ASS54 and make the alterations indicated.
Text to be arranged in 2 columns - 75 mm wide; 10 mm space between.
Page 1 - 25 mm left margin; 25 mm right margin; 30 mm bottom margin.
Page 2 - 25 mm left margin; 25 mm right margin; top margin 30 mm.
Type specifications - Palatino 16 point.
Add a header (embolden) on page 1 as shown 10 mm from top edge of paper (Palatino 14 point).
Horizontal lines (1 point) to begin and end in alignment with text.
Vertical space between lines to be 15 mm.
Main heading - *CHAIRMAN'S STATEMENT* - to commence 50 mm from top edge of paper.
INTRODUCTION to commence 70 mm from top edge of paper.
Centre page numbers 10 mm from bottom edge of paper.
Print one copy of both pages. Save as ASS58.

DDA STORES PLC - The Impact of DO IT YOURSELF

HOME IMPROVEMENTS

Living Area

> ASSIGNMENT 59
> Instructions on following page.

Great scope exists for the householder to improve the decor within the living areas of the home. Wall papering, painting, wood cladding, plastering and door replacement are all areas where the homeowner can make considerable savings both in time and money. Suppliers are only too willing to offer suggestions both in the method of construction and in the design of the living areas. This not only reassures the individual but also can save time and extra expense.

The quality of self-assembly furniture has given even wider scope for the individual and a wide range of furniture can be purchased and assembled using only the minimum of tools. In all self-assembly packs, the instructions are clear and concise.

Kitchen Area

Although many householders will engage professional help when installing a new kitchen, it is nevertheless possible to design and purchase units for the kitchen area from the DIY store. Considerable time and care should be taken, however, when measuring for wall units and cupboards. Problems can arise when wall measurements do not correspond to the unit sizes. Here again, however, the DIY enthusiast can undertake such a project knowing that expert advice and hints are readily available from the supplier.

Improving the kitchen is probably the most value-adding improvement which can be made within the home. Considering the amount of time spent in this area, it will also be one of the first areas of the home to be upgraded. Built-in or freestanding appliances can be costly additions to the kitchen but the majority of homes will have such appliances as the washing machine, tumble dryer, dishwasher, fridge or freezer and a microwave oven.

Bathroom Area

A replacement bathroom will be determined by not only your

current needs, but also the likely future requirements for the area. Modern bathroom equipment is available from the DIY store in a wide choice of styles, shapes and colours. Planning the bathroom is critical since this can often be the smallest area in the home. Will the size and shape of the room allow for the installation of both a bath and a separate shower?

Pedestal basins are available in various sizes and shapes and can be either wall mounted or can be fitted in a corner. The WC cistern can often be concealed behind the wall thus adding to the available space within the bathroom. Apart from these basic items, some consideration must be given to the lighting within the bathroom. If in doubt, call in the experts.

DIY has become popular in British households over the last decade. Fifteen years ago, the householder would call in the experts be they plumbers, plasterers, painters or joiners. Today it is not uncommon for both the man and the woman of the household to undertake tasks around the house. By offering a wide choice, competitive prices and convenient shopping hours,

DIY stores have contributed greatly to the popularity of DO IT YOURSELF.

ASSIGNMENT 59
Recall ASS55 and make the alterations indicated.
Text to be arranged in 2 columns - 70 mm wide; 15 mm space between.
Page 1 - 30 mm left margin; 25 mm right margin; 25 mm bottom margin.
Page 2 - 25 mm left margin; 30 mm right margin; top margin 25 mm.
Type specifications - AvantGarde 14 point.
Add a header (embolden) on page 1 as shown 10 mm from top edge of paper (AvantGarde 16 point).
Horizontal lines (0.5 point) to begin and end in alignment with text.
Vertical space between lines to be 20 mm.
Main heading - **HOME IMPROVEMENTS** - to commence 40 mm from top edge of paper.
Living Area to commence 50 mm from top edge of paper.
Centre page numbers 15 mm from bottom edge of paper.
Print one copy of both pages. Save as ASS59.

LYMAC Golf and Leisure Promotion

GOLF - "THE LYMAC WAY"

General Information

> ASSIGNMENT 60
> Instructions on following page.

With the increasing amount of leisure time that is given to the general business community, it is important that this additional time is spent in a wise, healthy and enjoyable way. There's no better way to utilise this time than to participate in the art of "The Royal and Ancient Game". Lymac Golf and Leisure Promotion can offer a wide variety of options that will cater for all ages, male or female in the world of golf. Our aim is to provide our clients with the opportunity to play quality golf courses, obtain professional tuition, have fun and pleasure - all at affordable prices. We will also provide "off-the-course" entertainment for all of our clients, their families and guests while under contract with Lymac.

Courses

Lymac Golf and Leisure Promotion have acquired the reputation of being able to promote one of the largest selections of golf course availability to their clients. Over the last 15 years we have been able to achieve an unbeatable success rate in obtaining access to some of the most famous golfing links in a number of countries. Lymac concentrates its promotional activities at "the home of golf" - Scotland, but can also facilitate requests for other courses in the United Kingdom and indeed the remainder of Europe. As yet, we have not moved into the full international golfing arena, but plans are well ahead to enter into the United States of America in the next 2 years.

Leave the arrangements to us - we have the drive to book the course of your choice.

Equipment

Don't let the lack of equipment or difficulty of travel stand in your way - Lymac offer a full range of equipment-hire from a basic half-set of irons to tournament-grade clubs, bags, balls, trolleys and even electric "buggies" in your package. All the major suppliers of golf equipment are on contract with Lymac and we will guarantee to supply the equipment of your choice on request. As well as providing the hire of equipment, we will also supply each golfer with a Lymac Presentation Pack (free of charge). Each pack contains 6 golf balls, a golf glove, tees, markers and a club tie - all items have the Lymac logo. Should you require any additional items which have not been listed please contact our representative who will be happy to make the necessary arrangements to meet your requirements. We aim to please every golfer who registers with our firm and aim to make the choice of outing a time to remember.

If you want to be on par with the professionals - contact Lymac.

ASSIGNMENT 60
Recall ASS56 and make the alterations indicated.
Text to be arranged in 2 columns - 75 mm wide; 10 mm space between.
Page 1 - 25 mm left margin; 25 mm right margin; 30 mm bottom margin.
Page 2 - 25 mm left margin; 25 mm right margin; top margin 15 mm.
Type specifications - Palatino 18 point.
Add a header (embolden) on page 1 as shown 10 mm from top edge of paper (Palatino 18 point).
Horizontal lines (1 point) to begin and end in alignment with text.
Vertical space between lines to be 15 mm.
Main heading - **_GOLF - "THE LYMAC WAY"_** - to commence 50 mm from top edge of paper.
General Information to commence 60 mm from top edge of paper.
Centre page numbers 10 mm from bottom edge of paper.
Print one copy of both pages. Save as ASS60.

A & D TOURS PLC - Chairman's Statement

CHAIRMAN'S STATEMENT

INTRODUCTION

Last year has seen a remarkable growth in our business to the extent that we have increased our sales force by 5 per cent to cope with the increased demand for our product. In recent years the demand for vacations has increased - customers are now taking short breaks as well as the traditional summer vacations. Our Management Team has improved the service to the customers by offering a wide and varied selection of reasonably priced holidays and the customer has responded by demanding better accommodation, better meals and improved travel arrangements. All of these have been taken on board by the Management Team and this has resulted in an increase in sales in what must be considered to be "an expanding market".

RESULTS

I am pleased to report to our stockholders that earnings per share have increased by 28 per cent. This has enabled us to declare a final dividend of 3.55 pence, giving an overall increase for the year of 10.5 per cent. This increase is the highest for a number of years and it indicates the confidence which exists within our Company. We are determined to increase the efficiency of our activities within the Company over the next 3 years.

Our Management Team is strong with many new proposals coming forward for a maintenance of our market position. We aim to target Short Breaks next year with the emphasis being on an improved option choice within Scotland. We also aim to improve the selection of European locations for both short and long stay holidays.

The Board has agreed that the Marketing section should be strengthened and that the principal focus will be on the areas mentioned above. We shall be making substantial

---

ASSIGNMENT 61
Instructions on following page.

investments in our Short Break hotel chain and we intend to improve the profitability of a number of our European hotels, particularly in Spain. We are also exploring and evaluating opportunities for profitable growth in Germany and Italy.

Economic conditions fluctuated considerably over the last 12 months and this had a direct influence on our results for the period. In spite of these conditions, I am pleased to report a satisfactory performance.

I am confident that we can exploit the growth opportunities which these offer.

BOARD

Two new Directors have been appointed recently. Mrs Hilary Whyte has extensive knowledge of European holidays and Mr John Black brings extensive experience and knowledge of the home market.

Mrs Marion Duncan and Mr James Clive retired from the Board and we wish them well in their retirement.

The names of the Directors of the Company are shown on page 29 of the Annual Report. Mr Peter Johnstone, Mrs Joan Brownlee and Dr Robert Fleming will retire by rotation at the Annual General Meeting and offer themselves for re-election.

Mrs Pauline Hogarth and Dr William Russell were appointed Directors last year and they will retire at the Annual General Meeting and offer themselves for election.

ASSIGNMENT 61
Recall ASS53 and make the alterations indicated.
Text to be arranged in 3 columns - 70 mm wide; 15 mm space between.
25 mm left margin; 25 mm right margin; 25 mm bottom margin.
Top margin - Page 2 - 50 mm.
Type specifications - AvantGarde 14 point.
Add a header (embolden) on page 1 as shown 10 mm from top edge of paper (AvantGarde 16 point).
Horizontal lines (0.5 point) to begin and end in alignment with text.
Vertical space between lines to be 20 mm.
Main heading - **CHAIRMAN'S STATEMENT** - to commence 40 mm from top edge of paper.
INTRODUCTION to commence 50 mm from top edge of paper.
Centre page numbers 15 mm from bottom edge of paper.
Print one copy of both pages. Save as ASS61.

ALDON FINANCIAL SERVICES PLC - Chairman's Statement

CHAIRMAN'S STATEMENT

ASSIGNMENT 62
Instructions on following page.

INTRODUCTION

I am pleased to announce pre-tax profits for the year of £696 million. This is an increase of 6% on last year's figures. The post-tax figures for the current year have also shown a slight increase (1.5%) to £294 million which has covered the proposed dividend allowance for shareholders. As you will no doubt be aware the current market conditions, although slow, have improved and the prospects for next year appear to be brighter than first anticipated for our financial institution. Indeed, I would suggest that our organisation is in a much stronger position than many of our foreign competitors. This must be encouraging news for our shareholders and our customers alike.

Customers remain to be our top priority and this is reflected in the proposals and recommendations for the future as laid out in the Annual Report and Accounts.

Despite the previous financial year being difficult for most financial institutions, Aldon Financial Services PLC retained its share price and ended the year 9% above the FT All-Share Index (the third consecutive year that Aldon's Share Price has been above this index).

Once again there was no call on shareholders (for the eighteenth consecutive year) and the dividend was increased by 11% on last year's figures. This development of progressive increases keeps our organisation in line with the Board's objective stated in the strategic plan "to produce shareholders' long-term, superior total returns, comprising continued dividend growth and appreciation in the share price".

In spite of both economic and competitive conditions the

performance of our organisation retains our position in the Financial Services sector.

BOARD

Since last year's report the Board have seen a number of changes. Two new members have been welcomed to the Board.

Mr Kenneth McDonald joined us in November of last year as Senior Executive and Miss Eileen Fraser was appointed in February as Financial Controller (Foreign Investment). Mr Johnston Forsyth will be retiring at the forthcoming Annual General Meeting. Mr Forsyth joined the Board in 1976 and was Vice Chairman from 1981 to 1987. He has made a significant contribution to the organisation over many years, for which we, the Board are extremely grateful. I take this opportunity of wishing him a healthy and happy retirement.

STAFF

Our Management Staff have had a difficult year with the introduction of new management techniques. They have had to participate in many new aspects of organisational procedures and evaluation exercises over the last financial year. I am sure these new initiatives will be welcomed by staff at all levels in the very near future. On behalf of the Board I thank them for their continued effort and support.

ASSIGNMENT 62
Recall ASS54 and make the alterations indicated.
Text to be arranged in 3 columns - 75 mm wide; 10 mm space between.
25 mm left margin; 25 mm right margin; 30 mm bottom margin.
Top margin - Page 2 - 70 mm.
Type specifications - Palatino 14 point.
Add a header (embolden) on page 1 as shown 10 mm from top edge of paper (Palatino 17 point).
Horizontal lines (1 point) to begin and end in alignment with text.
Vertical space between lines to be 15 mm.
Main heading - *CHAIRMAN'S STATEMENT* - to commence 50 mm from top edge of paper.
INTRODUCTION to commence 70 mm from top edge of paper.
Centre page numbers 15 mm from bottom edge of paper.
Print one copy of both pages. Save as ASS62.

DDA STORES PLC - The Impact of DO IT YOURSELF

HOME IMPROVEMENTS

ASSIGNMENT 63
Instructions on following page.

Living Area

Great scope exists for the householder to improve the decor within the living areas of the home. Wall papering, painting, wood cladding, plastering and door replacement are all areas where the homeowner can make considerable savings both in time and money. Suppliers are only too willing to offer suggestions both in the method of construction and in the design of the living areas. This not only reassures the individual but also can save time and extra expense.

The quality of self-assembly furniture has given even wider scope for the individual and a wide range of furniture can be purchased and assembled using only the minimum of tools. In all self-assembly packs, the instructions are clear and concise.

Kitchen Area

Although many householders will engage professional help when installing a new kitchen, it is nevertheless possible to design and purchase units for the kitchen area from the DIY store. Considerable time and care should be taken, however, when measuring for wall units and cupboards. Problems can arise when wall measurements do not correspond to the unit sizes. Here again, however, the DIY enthusiast can undertake such a project knowing that expert advice and hints are readily available from the supplier.

Improving the kitchen is probably the most value-adding improvement which can be made within the home. Considering the amount of time spent in this area, it will also be one of the first areas of the home to be upgraded. Built-in or freestanding appliances can be costly additions to the kitchen but the majority of homes will have such appliances as the washing machine, tumble dryer, dishwasher, fridge or freezer and a microwave oven.

to the popularity of DO IT YOURSELF.

ASSIGNMENT 63
Recall ASS55 and make the alterations indicated.
Text to be arranged in 3 columns - 70 mm wide; 15 mm space between.
25 mm left margin; 25 mm right margin; 25 mm bottom margin.
Top margin - Page 2 - 50 mm.
Type specifications - AvantGarde 14 point.
Add a header (embolden) on page 1 as shown 10 mm from top edge of paper (AvantGarde 16 point).
Horizontal lines (0.5 point) to begin and end in alignment with text.
Vertical space between lines to be 20 mm.
Main heading - **HOME IMPROVEMENTS** - to commence 40 mm from top edge of paper.
Living Area to commence 50 mm from top edge of paper.
Centre page numbers 15 mm from bottom edge of paper.
Print one copy of both pages. Save as ASS63.

Bathroom Area

A replacement bathroom will be determined by not only your current needs, but also the likely future requirements for the area. Modern bathroom equipment is available from the DIY store in a wide choice of styles, shapes and colours. Planning the bathroom is critical since this can often be the smallest area in the home. Will the size and shape of the room allow for the installation of both a bath and a separate shower?

Pedestal basins are available in various sizes and shapes and can be either wall mounted or can be fitted in a corner. The WC cistern can often be concealed behind the wall thus adding to the available space within the bathroom. Apart from these basic items, some consideration must be given to the lighting within the bathroom. If in doubt, call in the experts.

DIY has become popular in British households over the last decade. Fifteen years ago, the householder would call in the experts be they plumbers, plasterers, painters or joiners. Today it is not uncommon for both the man and the woman of the household to undertake tasks around the house. By offering a wide choice, competitive prices and convenient shopping hours, DIY stores have contributed greatly

78

2

LYMAC Golf and Leisure Promotion

> ASSIGNMENT 64
> Instructions on following page.

GOLF - "THE LYMAC WAY"

General Information

With the increasing amount of leisure time that is given to the general business community, it is important that this additional time is spent in a wise, healthy and enjoyable way. There's no better way to utilise this time than to participate in the art of "The Royal and Ancient Game". Lymac Golf and Leisure Promotion can offer a wide variety of options that will cater for all ages, male or female in the world of golf. Our aim is to provide our clients with the opportunity to play quality golf courses, obtain professional tuition, have fun and pleasure - all at affordable prices. We will also provide "off-the-course" entertainment for all of our clients, their families and guests while under contract with Lymac.

Courses

Lymac Golf and Leisure Promotion have acquired the reputation of being able to promote one of the largest selections of golf course availability to their clients. Over the last 15 years we have been able to achieve an unbeatable success rate in obtaining access to some of the most famous golfing links in a number of countries. Lymac concentrates its promotional activities at "the home of golf" - Scotland, but can also facilitate requests for other courses in the United Kingdom and indeed the remainder of Europe. As yet, we have not moved into the full international golfing arena, but plans are well ahead to enter into the United States of America in the next 2 years.

Leave the arrangements to us - we have the drive to book the course of your choice.

Equipment

Don't let the lack of equipment or difficulty of travel stand in your way - Lymac offer a full range of equipment-hire from a basic half-set of irons to tournament-grade clubs, bags, balls, trolleys and even electric "buggies" in your package. All the major suppliers of golf equipment are on contract with Lymac and we will guarantee to supply the equipment of your choice on request. As well as providing the hire of equipment, we will also supply each golfer with a Lymac Presentation Pack (free of charge). Each pack contains 6 golf balls, a golf glove, tees, markers and a club tie - all items have the Lymac logo. Should you require any additional items which have not been listed please contact our representative who will be happy to make the necessary arrangements to meet your requirements. We aim to please every golfer who registers with our firm and aim to make the choice of outing a time to remember.

If you want to be on par with the professionals - contact Lymac.

ASSIGNMENT 64
Recall ASS56 and make the alterations indicated.
Text to be arranged in 3 columns - 75 mm wide; 10 mm space between.
25 mm left margin; 25 mm right margin; 30 mm bottom margin.
Top margin - Page 2 - 70 mm.
Type specifications - Palatino 15 point.
Add a header (embolden) on page 1 as shown 10 mm from top edge of paper (Palatino 17 point).
Horizontal lines (1 point) to begin and end in alignment with text.
Vertical space between lines to be 15 mm.
Main heading - ***GOLF - "THE LYMAC WAY"*** - to commence 50 mm from top edge of paper.
<u>General Information</u> to commence 70 mm from top edge of paper.
Centre page numbers 10 mm from bottom edge of paper.
Print one copy of both pages. Save as ASS64.

A & D TOURS PLC - Chairman's Statement

> ASSIGNMENT 65
> Instructions on following page.

CHAIRMAN'S STATEMENT

INTRODUCTION

Last year has seen a remarkable growth in our business to the extent that we have increased our sales force by 5 per cent to cope with the increased demand for our product. In recent years the demand for vacations has increased - customers are now taking short breaks as well as the traditional summer vacations. Our Management Team has improved the service to the customers by offering a wide and varied selection of reasonably priced holidays and the customer has responded by demanding better accommodation, better meals and improved travel arrangements. All of these have been taken on board by the Management Team and this has resulted in an increase in sales in what must be considered to be "an expanding market".

RESULTS

I am pleased to report to our stockholders that earnings per share have increased by 28 per cent. This has enabled us to declare a final dividend of 3.55 pence, giving an overall increase for the year of 10.5 per cent. This increase is the highest for a number of years and it indicates the confidence which exists within our Company. We are determined to increase the efficiency of our activities within the Company over the next 3 years.

Our Management Team is strong with many new proposals coming forward for a maintenance of our market position. We aim to target Short Breaks next year with the emphasis being on an improved option choice within Scotland. We also aim to improve the selection of European locations for both short and long stay holidays.

The Board has agreed that the Marketing section should be strengthened and that the principal focus will be on the areas mentioned above. We shall be

ASSIGNMENT 65
Recall ASS53 and make the alterations indicated.
Text to be on A4 landscape in 4 columns - text space 45 mm wide; 8 mm space between, 50 mm between columns 2 and 3.
25 mm left margin; 26 mm right margin; 25 mm bottom margin. Top margin - Page 2 - 50 mm. Type specifications - AvantGarde 13 point.
Add a header (embolden and centre) on page 1 as shown 10 mm from top edge of paper (AvantGarde 16 point).
Horizontal lines (0.5 point) to begin and end in alignment with text. Vertical space between lines to be 20 mm.
Main heading - **CHAIRMAN'S STATEMENT** - to commence 40 mm from top edge of paper.
INTRODUCTION to commence 50 mm from top edge of paper. Remove page numbers. Print one copy of both pages. Save as ASS65.

---

making substantial investments in our Short Break hotel chain and we intend to improve the profitability of a number of our European hotels, particularly in Spain. We are also exploring and evaluating opportunities for profitable growth in Germany and Italy.

Economic conditions fluctuated considerably over the last 12 months and this had a direct influence on our results for the period. In spite of these conditions, I am pleased to report a

satisfactory performance.

I am confident that we can exploit the growth opportunities which these offer.

BOARD

Two new Directors have been appointed recently. Mrs Hilary Whyte has extensive knowledge of European holidays and Mr John Black brings extensive experience and knowledge of the home market.

Mrs Marion Duncan and Mr James Clive retired from the Board

and we wish them well in their retirement.

The names of the Directors of the Company are shown on page 29 of the Annual Report. Mr Peter Johnstone, Mrs Joan Brownlee and Dr Robert Fleming will retire by rotation at the Annual General Meeting and offer themselves for re-election.

Mrs Pauline Hogarth and Dr William Russell were appointed Directors last year and they will retire at the Annual General Meeting and offer

themselves for election.

ALDON FINANCIAL SERVICES PLC - Chairman's Statement

CHAIRMAN'S STATEMENT

ASSIGNMENT 66
Instructions on following page.

INTRODUCTION

I am pleased to announce pre-tax profits for the year of £696 million. This is an increase of 6% on last year's figures. The post-tax figures for the current year have also shown a slight increase (1.5%) to £294 million which has covered the proposed dividend allowance for shareholders. As you will no doubt be aware the current market conditions, although slow, have improved and the prospects for next year appear to be brighter than first anticipated for our financial institution. Indeed, I would suggest that our organisation is in a much stronger position than many of our foreign competitors. This must be encouraging news for our shareholders and our customers alike.

Customers remain to be our top priority and this is reflected in the proposals and recommendations for the future as laid out in the Annual Report and Accounts.

Despite the previous financial year being difficult for most financial institutions, Aldon Financial Services PLC retained its share price and ended the year 9% above the FT All-Share Index (the third consecutive year that Aldon's Share Price has been above this index). Once again there was no call on shareholders (for the eighteenth consecutive year) and the dividend was increased by 11% on last year's figures. This development of progressive increases keeps our organisation in line with the objective stated in the Board's strategic plan "to produce shareholders' long-term, superior

ASSIGNMENT 66
Recall ASS54 and make the alterations indicated.
Text to be on A4 landscape in 4 columns - text space 50 mm; 12 mm space between, 36 mm between columns 2 and 3.
18 mm left margin; 19 mm right margin. Top margin - Page 2 - 70 mm.
Type specifications - Palatino 14 point.
Add a header (embolden and centre) on page 1 as shown 10 mm from top edge of paper (Palatino 16 point).
Horizontal lines (1 point) to begin and end in alignment with text. Vertical space between lines to be 15 mm.
Main heading - *CHAIRMAN'S STATEMENT* - to commence 50 mm from top edge of paper.
INTRODUCTION to commence 70 mm from top edge of paper. Bottom margin 30 mm.
Remove page numbers. Print one copy of both pages. Save as ASS66.

---

total returns, comprising continued dividend growth and appreciation in the share price".

In spite of both economic and competitive conditions the performance of our organisation retains our position in the Financial Services sector.

BOARD

Since last year's report the Board have seen a number of changes. Two new members have been welcomed to the Board.

Mr Kenneth McDonald joined us in November of last year as Senior Executive and Miss Eileen Fraser was appointed in February as Financial Controller (Foreign Investment). Mr Johnston Forsyth will be retiring at the forthcoming Annual General Meeting. Mr Forsyth joined the Board in 1976 and was Vice Chairman from 1981 to 1987. He has made a significant contribution to the organisation over many years, for which we, the Board are extremely grateful. I take this opportunity of wishing him a healthy and happy retirement.

STAFF

Our Management Staff have had a difficult year with the introduction of new management techniques. They have had to participate in many new aspects of organisational procedures and evaluation exercises over the last financial year. I am sure these new initiatives will be welcomed by staff at all levels in the very near future. On behalf of the Board I thank them for their continued effort and support.

DDA STORES PLC - The Impact of DO IT YOURSELF

HOME IMPROVEMENTS

Living Area

Great scope exists for the householder to improve the decor within the living areas of the home. Wall papering, painting, wood cladding, plastering and door replacement are all areas where the homeowner can make considerable savings both in time and money. Suppliers are only too willing to offer suggestions both in the method of construction and in the design of the living areas. This not only reassures the individual but also can save time and extra expense.

The quality of self-assembly furniture has given even wider scope for the individual and a wide range of furniture can be purchased and assembled using only the minimum of tools. In all self-assembly packs, the instructions are clear and concise.

Kitchen Area

Although many householders will engage professional help when installing a new kitchen, it is nevertheless possible to design and purchase units for the kitchen area from the DIY store. Considerable time and care should be taken, however, when measuring for wall units and cupboards. Problems can arise when wall measurements do not correspond to the unit sizes. Here again, however, the DIY enthusiast can undertake such a project knowing that expert advice and hints are readily available from the supplier.

Improving the kitchen is probably the most value-adding improvement which can be made within the home. Considering the amount of time spent in this area, it will also be one of the first areas of the home to be upgraded. Built-in or freestanding appliances can be costly additions to the kitchen but the majority of homes

> ASSIGNMENT 67
> Instructions on following page.

85

ASSIGNMENT 67
Recall ASS55 and make the alterations indicated.
Text to be on A4 landscape in 4 columns - text space 45 mm wide; 8 mm space between, 50 mm between columns 2 and 3.
25 mm left margin; 26 mm right margin; 25 mm bottom margin. Top margin - Page 2 - 50 mm. Type specifications - AvantGarde 14 point.
Add a header (embolden and centre) on page 1 as shown 10 mm from top edge of paper (AvantGarde 16 point).
Horizontal lines (0.5 point) to begin and end in alignment with text. Vertical space between lines to be 20 mm.
Main heading - **HOME IMPROVEMENTS** - to commence 40 mm from top edge of paper.
Living Area to commence 50 mm from top edge of paper. Bottom margin 17 mm. Remove page numbers. Print one copy of both pages. Save as ASS67.

will have such appliances as the washing machine, tumble dryer, dishwasher, fridge or freezer and a microwave oven.

Bathroom Area

A replacement bathroom will be determined by not only your current needs, but also the likely future requirements for the area. Modern b a t h r o o m equipment is available from the DIY store in a wide choice of styles, shapes and colours.

Planning the bathroom is critical since this can often be the smallest area in the home. Will the size and shape of the room allow for the installation of both a bath and a separate shower?

Pedestal basins are available in various sizes and shapes and can be either wall mounted or can be fitted in a corner. The WC cistern can often be concealed behind the wall thus adding to the available space within the bathroom. Apart from these basic items, some consideration must be given to the lighting within the bathroom. If in doubt, call in the experts.

DIY has become popular in British households over the last decade. Fifteen years ago, the householder would call in the experts be they p l u m b e r s , plasterers, painters or joiners. Today it is not uncommon for both the man and the woman of the household to undertake tasks around the house. By offering a wide c h o i c e , competitive prices and convenient shopping hours, DIY stores have contributed greatly to the popularity of DO IT YOURSELF.

LYMAC Golf and Leisure Promotion

ASSIGNMENT 68
Instructions on following page.

GOLF - "THE LYMAC WAY"

General Information

With the increasing amount of leisure time that is given to the general business community, it is important that this additional time is spent in a wise, healthy and enjoyable way. There's no better way to utilise this time than to participate in the art of "The Royal and Ancient Game". Lymac Golf and Leisure Promotion can offer a wide variety of options that will cater for all ages, male or female in the world of golf. Our aim is to provide our clients with the opportunity to play quality golf courses, obtain professional tuition, have fun and pleasure - all at affordable prices. We will also provide "off-the-course" entertainment for all of our clients, their families and guests while under contract with Lymac.

Courses

Lymac Golf and Leisure Promotion have acquired the reputation of being able to promote one of the largest selections of golf course availability to their clients. Over the last 15 years we have been able to achieve an unbeatable success rate in obtaining access to some of the most famous golfing links in a number of countries. Lymac concentrates its promotional activities at "the home of golf" - Scotland, but can also facilitate requests for other courses in the United Kingdom and indeed the remainder of Europe. As yet, we have not moved into

ASSIGNMENT 68

Recall ASS56 and make the alterations indicated.
Text to be on A4 landscape in 4 columns - text space 50 mm; 12 mm space between, 36 mm between columns 2 and 3. 18 mm left margin; 19 mm right margin. Top margin - Page 2 - 70 mm.
Type specifications - Palatino 15 point.
Add a header (embolden and centre) on page 1 as shown 10 mm from top edge of paper (Palatino 18 point).
Horizontal lines (1 point) to begin and end in alignment with text. Vertical space between lines to be 15 mm.
Main heading - *GOLF - "THE LYMAC WAY"* - to commence 50 mm from top edge of paper.
General Information to commence 70 mm from top edge of paper. Bottom margin 30 mm.
Remove page numbers. Print one copy of both pages. Save as ASS68.

---

the full international golfing arena, but plans are well ahead to enter into the United States of America in the next 2 years.

Leave the arrangements to us - we have the drive to book the course of your choice.

Equipment

Don't let the lack of equipment or difficulty of travel stand in your way - Lymac offer a full range of equipment-hire from a basic half-set of irons to tournament-grade clubs, bags, balls, trolleys and even electric "buggies" in your package. All the major suppliers of golf equipment are on contract with Lymac and we will guarantee to supply the equipment of your choice on request. As well as providing the hire of equipment, we will also supply each golfer with a Lymac Presentation Pack (free of charge). Each pack contains 6 golf balls, a golf glove, tees, markers and a club tie - all items have the Lymac logo. Should you require any additional items which have not been listed please contact our representative who will be happy to make the necessary arrangements to meet your requirements. We aim to please every golfer who registers with our firm and aim to make the choice of outing a time to remember.

If you want to be on par with the professionals - contact Lymac.

A & D TOURS PLC - Chairman's Statement

CHAIRMAN'S STATEMENT

INTRODUCTION

> ASSIGNMENT 69
> Recall ASS57 and add the text - FUTURE OUTLOOK to ". . . year with optimism." before the BOARD section.
> Print one copy of all pages. Save as ASS69.

Last year has seen a remarkable growth in our business to the extent that we have increased our sales force by 5 per cent to cope with the increased demand for our product. In recent years the demand for vacations has increased - customers are now taking short breaks as well as the traditional summer vacations. Our Management Team has improved the service to the customers by offering a wide and varied selection of reasonably priced holidays and the customer has responded by demanding better accommodation, better meals and improved travel arrangements. All of these have been taken on board by the Management Team and this has resulted in an increase in sales in what must be considered to be "an expanding market".

RESULTS

I am pleased to report to our stockholders that earnings per share have increased by 28 per cent. This has enabled us to declare a final dividend of 3.55 pence, giving an overall increase for the year of 10.5 per cent. This increase is the highest for a number of years and it indicates the confidence which exists within our Company. We are determined to increase the efficiency of our activities within the Company over the next 3 years.

Our Management Team is strong with many new proposals coming forward for a maintenance of our market position. We aim to target Short Breaks next year with the emphasis being on an improved option choice within Scotland. We also aim to improve the selection of European locations for both short and long stay holidays.

The Board has agreed that the Marketing section should be strengthened and that the principal focus will be on the areas mentioned above. We shall be making substantial investments in our Short Break hotel chain and we intend to improve the profitability of a number of our European hotels, particularly in Spain. We are also exploring and evaluating opportunities for profitable growth in Germany and Italy.

Economic conditions fluctuated considerably over the last 12 months and this had a direct influence on our results for the period. In spite of these conditions, I am pleased to report a satisfactory performance.

I am confident that we can exploit the growth opportunities which these offer.

FUTURE OUTLOOK

The reduction of debt within our company was a main financial objective this year and we have had considerable success in this area by prudent cash management and by careful selection of hotels and holiday packages within the United Kingdom.

In the current economic climate, it is not surprising that our customers are making cost a priority and many are choosing to delay their final choice until "late bargains" appear.

Considerable effort will require to be made to ensure that next year's customers will be attracted to our packages at an earlier date and every incentive must be investigated to encourage them to make confirmed bookings. Cash reductions, payment of insurance, extended breaks, gifts and future discounts must all be possible incentives and these will require to be widely advertised.

Figures for the last quarter are extremely promising and this would suggest that we can now expect to make significant progress towards the end of this year and hopefully this should create cash inflows which will allow us to meet our objectives.

We must constantly strive to conserve resources and minimise overheads. A review of our sales and marketing divisions will be undertaken within the next 6 months. Staff training will be given priority and to this end a new training section will be established within the Manchester branch.

We must also make the most effective use of modern technology. As you know, we have now equipped all of our branches with the latest computers thus allowing us to give an improved service to our customers. Customers will now be able to make instant bookings from a wide selection of holidays "at the touch of a button".

The installation and training have created minor problems but these have been identified throughout our branches and our investment has proved both attractive and beneficial to our customers. Our objective must be to offer customers a high standard of service which will not only encourage them to book with us today, but will also encourage them to come back to us next year and in the future.

Service to the general public takes many forms and we must strive to provide the best in available holiday listings and staff training as well as being able to offer the best possible financial packages.

The completed refurbishment of our branches in Edinburgh, Newcastle, Manchester, Belfast and Cardiff will allow us to make further economies. When existing schemes are completed, there will be a reduction in cash commitment.

The past year has been one of considerable progress for our overseas division. We have been able to improve profits by increasing revenue and cutting costs despite being in an area of considerable competition from other suppliers of holidays.

We have been able to make significant progress in restructuring our overseas organisation team and it is now considered that levels of staffing, research, consultants and locations are now at the correct level. The restructuring has reduced staffing levels from 220 to 184 and this has contributed to cost reductions over the year.

The training of young persons will be actively encouraged within the company and to this end, we will increase the number of training places from 26 to 42 next year.

Support will also be given to encourage existing staff to improve their formal qualifications by undertaking courses of study at their local College. National qualifications are readily available and it must be in the individual's (as well as the company's) interest to improve standards of education. The benefits to the company are significant and advantages must accrue from having a well motivated and highly qualified group of staff. The skills of disabled persons should continue to be recognised and we should do our utmost to encourage them within the company.

We will continue to strengthen our team as and when required but I have every faith in the existing team being able to lead the company into yet another successful and profitable year.

Finally I would like to take this opportunity of thanking all our management and staff within the company for their outstanding efforts during this fairly difficult year. I look forward to next year with optimisim.

BOARD

Two new Directors have been appointed recently. Mrs Hilary Whyte has extensive knowledge of European holidays and Mr John Black brings extensive experience and knowledge of the home market.

Mrs Marion Duncan and Mr James Clive retired from the Board and we wish them well in their retirement.

The names of the Directors of the Company are shown on page 29 of the Annual Report. Mr Peter Johnstone, Mrs Joan Brownlee and Dr Robert Fleming will retire by rotation at the Annual General Meeting and offer themselves for re-election.

Mrs Pauline Hogarth and Dr William Russell were appointed Directors last year and they will retire at the Annual General Meeting and offer themselves for election.

ALDON FINANCIAL SERVICES PLC - Chairman's Statement

CHAIRMAN'S STATEMENT

> ASSIGNMENT 70
> Recall ASS58 and add the text - FUTURE DEVELOPMENT PROGRAMME and SPONSORSHIP sections to the end of the STAFF section.
> Print one copy of all pages. Save as ASS70.

INTRODUCTION

I am pleased to announce pre-tax profits for the year of £696 million. This is an increase of 6% on last year's figures. The post-tax figures for the current year have also shown a slight increase (1.5%) to £294 million which has covered the proposed dividend allowance for shareholders. As you will no doubt be aware the current market conditions, although slow, have improved and the prospects for next year appear to be brighter than first anticipated for our financial institution. Indeed, I would suggest that our organisation is in a much stronger position than many of our foreign competitors. This must be encouraging news for our shareholders and our customers alike.

Customers remain to be our top priority and this is reflected in the proposals and recommendations for the future as laid out in the Annual Report and Accounts.

Despite the previous financial year being difficult for most financial institutions, Aldon Financial Services PLC retained its share price and ended the year 9% above the FT All-Share Index (the third consecutive year that Aldon's Share Price has been above this index). Once again there was no call on shareholders (for the eighteenth consecutive year) and the dividend was increased by 11% on last year's figures. This development of progressive increases keeps our organisation in line with the objective stated in the Board's strategic plan "to produce shareholders' long-term, superior total returns, comprising continued dividend growth and appreciation in the share price".

In spite of both economic and competitive conditions the performance of our organisation retains our position in the Financial Services sector.

BOARD

Since last year's report the Board have seen a number of changes. Two new members have been welcomed to the Board.

Mr Kenneth McDonald joined us in November of last year as Senior Executive and Miss Eileen Fraser was appointed in February as Financial Controller (Foreign Investment). Mr Johnston Forsyth will be retiring at the forthcoming Annual General Meeting. Mr Forsyth joined the Board in 1976 and was Vice Chairman from 1981 to 1987. He has made a significant contribution to the organisation over many years, for which we, the Board are extremely grateful. I take this opportunity of wishing him a healthy and happy retirement.

STAFF

Our Management Staff have had a difficult year with the introduction of new management techniques. They have had to participate in many new aspects of organisational procedures and evaluation exercises over the last financial year. I am sure these new initiatives will be welcomed by staff at all levels in the very near future. On behalf of the Board I thank them for their continued effort and support.

FUTURE DEVELOPMENT PROGRAMME

Aldon Financial Services PLC, as a major financial force, has the responsibility towards its shareholders (all groups), staff, customers and indeed to the country's economy as a whole. It is therefore the aim and the duty of the Board to achieve and maintain a level of profits as well as balance the interests of all the categories mentioned previously.

The company therefore undertakes to increase investment in the home financial market with the object of achieving this stated aim as well as stimulating the Financial Services sector of the economy. Our development programme shows that we, as a public limited company, are committed to a 5-year programme of investment - £200m per annum will be invested from pre-tax profits or reserves in order to create a sound foundation from which to expand our range of financial services to all our current and potential shareholders and customers. A group of experts will monitor the progress of the investment programme to ensure that the return to the shareholder will continue in terms of dividend growth. I remain optimistic that this development programme will benefit many, if not all, of our client group and keep Aldon Financial Services PLC at the forefront of the Financial Services sector of the economy.

On behalf of the Board, may I express my thanks to you, the shareholders, for your continued support to our firm which has enabled us to progress from strength to strength over the last year and maintain a positive approach to the forthcoming year with optimism. We will consolidate on our previous experience to form the sound foundations upon which Aldon can build in the years ahead.

SPONSORSHIP

As well as investment in the economy, I am pleased to announce our continued commitment to sponsorship deals and packages throughout the world of sport and leisure activities. Aldon has just signed a sponsorship deal as the major sponsor of a leading international tennis tournament to be held during the summer of next year. This will be the fourth year in succession that we have been involved with this tournament but it will be the first time that we will be the main sponsor of the event.

A further feature of our

development programme is a recent addition of a package for the promotion and sponsorship of the "Sport for the Disabled Week" during the second week of March next year. This will be another "first" for Aldon and we are delighted to be involved in such an important national event for disabled sportsmen and sportswomen. We have signed a deal worth £75,000 for this event which will help to promote the event from the beginning of next year.

Although these are the 2 major sponsorship deals, we will continue to be involved in a number of other packages as well as entering into some new sponsorships to keep the name of Aldon Financial Services PLC in a high profile in the sport and leisure arena throughout the country for another year.

The Board can assure all shareholders that the return on investment of such sponsorship deals and packages has been extremely worthwhile and benefits the "sponsored event" directly in the short-term. You, the shareholders, benefit indirectly in the longer term as the Aldon image is widened and potential customers become a reality. This means that more investment is gained within the firm thus increasing profits.

The total budget for sponsorship in the coming year will be £2.2 million. We have employed Miss Caroline Houston as the marketing specialist in this area to oversee this expanding function within our company.

DDA STORES PLC - The Impact of DO IT YOURSELF

HOME IMPROVEMENTS

Living Area

> ASSIGNMENT 71
> Recall ASS 59 and add the text - "Garden Improvements" to ". . . in the supply of materials." before the final paragraph.
> Print one copy of all pages. Save as ASS71.

Great scope exists for the householder to improve the decor within the living areas of the home. Wall papering, painting, wood cladding, plastering and door replacement are all areas where the homeowner can make considerable savings both in time and money. Suppliers are only too willing to offer suggestions both in the method of construction and in the design of the living areas. This not only reassures the individual but also can save time and extra expense.

The quality of self-assembly furniture has given even wider scope for the individual and a wide range of furniture can be purchased and assembled using only the minimum of tools. In all self-assembly packs, the instructions are clear and concise.

Kitchen Area

Although many householders will engage professional help when installing a new kitchen, it is nevertheless possible to design and purchase units for the kitchen area from the DIY store. Considerable time and care should be taken, however, when measuring for wall units and cupboards. Problems can arise when wall measurements do not correspond to the unit sizes. Here again, however, the DIY enthusiast can undertake such a project knowing that expert advice and hints are readily available from the supplier.

Improving the kitchen is probably the most value-adding improvement which can be made within the home. Considering the amount of time spent in this area, it will also be one of the first areas of the home to be upgraded. Built-in or freestanding appliances can be costly additions to the kitchen but the majority of homes will have such appliances as the washing machine, tumble dryer, dishwasher, fridge or freezer and a microwave oven.

Bathroom Area

A replacement bathroom will be determined by not only your

current needs, but also the likely future requirements for the area. Modern bathroom equipment is available from the DIY store in a wide choice of styles, shapes and colours. Planning the bathroom is critical since this can often be the smallest area in the home. Will the size and shape of the room allow for the installation of both a bath and a separate shower?

Pedestal basins are available in various sizes and shapes and can be either wall mounted or can be fitted in a corner. The WC cistern can often be concealed behind the wall thus adding to the available space within the bathroom. Apart from these basic items, some consideration must be given to the lighting within the bathroom. If in doubt, call in the experts.

Garden Improvements

Most people enjoy sitting in the garden on a warm day during the summer.

The addition of a patio area can enhance any property and all the materials necessary for the completion of such a project are readily available at all of our stores throughout the country.

Some plan must be prepared before making any purchases and it is recommended that careful measurements are made and carefully noted. Any such development will add to the value of any property and will be an attractive feature in the garden.

Paving slabs are available in a wide range of size, colour, shape and surface.

You can choose from a wide range of natural colours - buff, grey, brown, yellow or slate. Many DIY enthusiasts will select a mixture of colours to give an appealing effect.

Sales of paving bricks have increased dramatically in recent months and many DIY persons are choosing these as an alternative to concrete slabs. They are small, easy to handle and can be arranged in a variety of patterns. Helpful information is always available from our building staff.

Double Glazing

A full range of quality double glazing for both windows and doors is now available from stock within our stores. There are many optional features and each pack comes with clear instructions for assembly. Heating costs have influenced many householders to invest in double glazing but quotations from double glazing firms may influence the DIY enthusiasts to tackle the project themselves.

There is a choice of wood, plastic or aluminium frames available and units will be prepared by our skilled glaziers.

Magnetic window framing is an alternative to the sealed units. The panel is easily fixed to the existing window frame and consequently saves considerable time and expense. The glazed panel can be easily removed for cleaning and can be opened to allow better air circulation within the room.

Perhaps the cheapest system is plastic film which comes in a variety of grades from a heavy duty plastic film to a fairly thin film. The latter should be used for small areas. The film is attached to the frame of the window and must be applied in warm weather so as to avoid any moisture being lodged between the film and the frame.

The choice is yours - you can spend as much or as little as you choose but make sure you select a style to match your existing windows as far as possible.

Central Heating

At all of our stores we have a large selection of radiators, boilers, thermostats etc - everything you might need to allow you to complete an installation. Planning of the heating system is obviously vital and we are able to supply you with details of recommended radiator sizes depending on the temperature required.

You will require to decide first of all on the type of fuel to be used. This may be governed by the fuel availability but care must be taken before a selection is made.

Some fuel systems are expensive to install but are comparatively cheap to run whereas some systems are relatively cheap to install but are comparatively expensive to operate.

Without proper insulation (especially in the loft) any central heating system will be expensive to operate and adequate care should be taken to ensure that the loft and the hot water cylinder are adequately insulated. Proper insulation will save money and it may also mean that the size of the system (including the boiler) can be reduced.

Proper control of the system must be a consideration and we can supply a variety of radiator thermostats and room thermostats which will control the operation of the boiler and pump.

A wide range of all the equipment necessary to complete your central heating system is available at all of our branches. Fitting the system is less complicated than you might imagine.

Remember - we have the knowledge and the expertise to assist with any difficulty whether it be at the initial planning stages or in the supply of materials.

DIY has become popular in British households over the last decade. Fifteen years ago, the householder would call in the experts be they plumbers, plasterers, painters or joiners. Today it is not uncommon for both the man and the woman of the household to undertake tasks around the house. By offering a wide choice, competitive prices and convenient shopping hours, DIY stores have contributed greatly to the popularity of DO IT YOURSELF.

LYMAC Golf and Leisure Promotion

GOLF - "THE LYMAC WAY"
General Information

> ASSIGNMENT 72
> Recall ASS60 and add the text - "<u>Competitions</u>" to "... outing with Lymac." after "... contact Lymac."
> Print one copy of all pages. Save as ASS72.

With the increasing amount of leisure time that is given to the general business community, it is important that this additional time is spent in a wise, healthy and enjoyable way. There's no better way to utilise this time than to participate in the art of "The Royal and Ancient Game". Lymac Golf and Leisure Promotion can offer a wide variety of options that will cater for all ages, male or female in the world of golf. Our aim is to provide our clients with the opportunity to play quality golf courses, obtain professional tuition, have fun and pleasure - all at affordable prices. We will also provide "off-the-course" entertainment for all of our clients, their families and guests while under contract with Lymac.

Courses

Lymac Golf and Leisure Promotion have acquired the reputation of being able to promote one of the largest selections of golf course availability to their clients. Over the last 15 years we have been able to achieve an unbeatable success rate in obtaining access to some of the most famous golfing links in a number of countries. Lymac concentrates its promotional activities at "the home of golf" - Scotland, but can also facilitate requests for other courses in the United Kingdom and indeed the

1

remainder of Europe. As yet, we have not moved into the full international golfing arena, but plans are well ahead to enter into the United States of America in the next 2 years.

Leave the arrangements to us - we have the drive to book the course of your choice.

Equipment

Don't let the lack of equipment or difficulty of travel stand in your way - Lymac offer a full range of equipment-hire from a basic half-set of irons to tournament-grade clubs, bags, balls, trolleys and even electric "buggies" in your package. All the major suppliers of golf equipment are on contract with Lymac and we will guarantee to supply the equipment of your choice on request. As well as providing the hire of equipment, we will also supply each golfer with a Lymac Presentation Pack (free of charge). Each pack contains 6 golf balls, a golf glove, tees, markers and a club tie - all items have the Lymac logo. Should you require any additional items which have not been listed please contact our representative who will be happy to make the necessary arrangements to meet your requirements. We aim to please every golfer who registers with our firm and aim to make the choice of outing a time to remember.

If you want to be on par with the professionals - contact Lymac.

Competitions

During your stay with Lymac, various voluntary competitions will be available for the full range of golfer from the complete beginner to the low or scratch golfer. A small entry fee will be charged to each competitor in order that prizes can be awarded at the end of each competition. All of these competitions are designed for fun and will follow different formats including for example, medal play, 2-ball foursomes, mixed foursomes, stableford and match-play events.

For the keen golfer, The Lymac Open Tournament is played over the course of your choice (provided that it meets the specifications laid down by Lymac) on the first Saturday in August each year. This 18-hole medal competition is open to all golfers male and female (from scratch to 18 handicap) and offers substantial cash prizes to the eventual winners of each handicap section.

For further details of all the above competitions contact Lina Donald our Sales Executive on 0334 21462 or 0334 21767/8/9.

Other Leisure Provisions

As well as catering for the golfer, Lymac have pleasure in offering alternative leisure pursuits for the "non-golfer" at all the locations advertised in our annual brochure.

Each hotel used by our firm has leisure club facilities including heated indoor swimming pool, whirlpool spa, sauna, sunbeds, steam room and a wide variety of exercise equipment for all ages. The full range of activities is offered free of charge to all our clients.

However, if you are not of a sporting nature, Lymac will arrange other acitivities including excursions to various places of interest during the day as well as cinema and theatre outings in the evening. (An extra charge per head will be made for these additional activities.)

Lymac also will keep your children amused during your stay as we have trained staff who will look after all children between 3 and 12 years of age. Activities during the day for children include swimming, mini golf, football, tennis, adventure playgrounds as well as a range of indoor games (all supervised by Lymac staff).

In the evening we will provide games and discos for the same age group as during the day. A babysitting/listening service is also available on request.

Lymac Golf and Leisure Promotion know how to make you and your party feel welcome and wish you a most enjoyable and relaxing holiday. Go home refreshed and ready to book your next outing with Lymac.

ASSIGNMENT 73
Recall ASS69 and display the text in 5 columns. Space between columns 10 mm.
Left, right, top and bottom margins to be 25 mm. Delete Header, Heading and page numbers.
Type specifications - AvantGarde 12 point. Print one copy of the first 2 pages. Save as ASS73.

INTRODUCTION

Last year has seen a remarkable growth in our business to the extent that we have increased our sales force by 5 per cent to cope with the increased demand for our product. In recent years the demand for vacations has increased - customers are now taking short breaks as well as the traditional summer vacations. Our Management Team has improved the service to the customers by offering a wide and varied selection of reasonably priced holidays and the customer has responded by demanding better accommodation, better meals and improved travel arrangements. All of these have been taken on board by the Management Team and this has resulted in an increase in sales in what must be considered to be "an expanding market".

RESULTS

I am pleased to report to our stockholders that earnings per share have increased by 28 per cent. This has enabled us to declare a final dividend of 3.55 pence, giving an overall increase for the year of 10.5 per cent. This increase is the highest for a number of years and it indicates the strengthened and determined Company. We are to increase the efficiency of our activities within the Company over the next 3 years.

Our Management Team is strong with many new proposals coming forward for a maintenance of our market position. We aim to target Short Breaks next year with the emphasis being on an improved option choice within Scotland. We also aim to improve the selection of European locations for both short and long stay holidays.

The Board has agreed that the principal focus will be on the areas mentioned above. We shall be making substantial investments in our Short Break hotel chain and we intend to improve the profitability of a number of our European hotels, particularly in Spain. We are also exploring and evaluating opportunities for profitable growth in Germany and Italy.

Economic conditions fluctuated considerably over the last 12 months and this had a direct influence on our results for the period. In spite of these conditions, I am pleased with the performance.

I am confident that we can exploit the growth opportunities which these offer.

FUTURE OUTLOOK

The reduction of debt within our company was a main financial objective this year and we have had considerable success in this area by prudent cash management and by careful selection of hotels and holiday packages within the United Kingdom.

In the current economic climate, it is not surprising that our customers are making cost a priority and many are

105

The past year has been one of considerable progress for our overseas division. We have been able to improve profits by increasing revenue and cutting costs despite being in an area of considerable competition from other suppliers of holidays.

We have been able to make significant progress in restructuring our overseas organisation team and it is now considered that levels of staffing, research, consultants and locations are now at the correct level. The restructuring has reduced staffing levels from 220 to 184 them to book with us today, but will also encourage them to come back to us next year and in the future.

Service to the general public takes many forms and we must strive to provide the best in available holiday listings and staff training as well as being able to offer the best possible financial packages.

The completed refurbishment of our branches in Edinburgh, Newcastle, Manchester, Belfast and Cardiff will allow us to make further economies. When existing schemes are completed, there will be a reduction in cash commitment.

know, we have now equipped all of our branches with the latest computers thus allowing us to give an improved service to our customers. Customers will now be able to make instant bookings from a wide selection of holidays "at the touch of a button".

We must constantly strive to conserve resources and minimise overheads. A review of our sales and marketing divisions will be undertaken within the next 6 months. Staff training will be given priority and to this end a new training section will be established within the Manchester branch.

The installation and training have created minor problems but these have been identified throughout our branches and our investment has proved both attractive and beneficial to our customers. Our objective must be to offer customers a high standard of service which will not only encourage

suggest that we can now expect to make significant progress towards the end of this year and hopefully this should create cash inflows which will allow us to meet our objectives.

Considerable effort will require to be made to ensure that next year's customers will be attracted to our packages at an earlier date and every incentive must be investigated to encourage them to make confirmed bookings. Cash reductions, payment of insurance, extended breaks, gifts and future discounts must all be possible incentives and these will require to be widely advertised.

Figures for the last quarter are extremely promising and this would choosing to delay their final choice until "late bargains" appear.

ASSIGNMENT 74
Recall ASS70 and display the text in 5 columns. Space between columns 10 mm.
Left, right, top and bottom margins to be 25 mm. Delete Header, Heading and page numbers.
Type specifications - Palatino 12 point. Print one copy of the first 2 pages. Save as ASS74.

INTRODUCTION

I am pleased to announce pre-tax profits for the year of £696 million. This is an increase of 6% on last year's figures. The post-tax figures for the current year have also shown a slight increase (1.5%) to £294 million which has covered the proposed dividend allowance for shareholders. As you will no doubt be aware the current market conditions, although slow, have improved and the prospects for next year appear to be brighter than first anticipated for our financial institution. Indeed, I would suggest that our organisation is in a much stronger position than many of our foreign competitors.

This must be encouraging news for our shareholders and our customers alike.

Customers remain to be our top priority and this is reflected in the proposals and recommendations for the future as laid out in the Annual Report and Accounts.

Despite the previous financial year being difficult for most financial institutions, Aldon Financial Services PLC retained its share price and ended the year 9% above the FT All-Share Index (the third consecutive year that Aldon's Share Price has been above this index). Once again there was no call on shareholders (for the eighteenth consecutive year) and increased by 11% on last year's figures. This development of progressive increases keeps our organisation in line with the Board's strategic plan "to produce shareholders' long-term, superior total returns, comprising continued dividend growth and appreciation in the share price".

In spite of both economic and competitive conditions the performance of our organisation retains our position in the Financial Services sector.

BOARD

Since last year's report the Board have seen a Two new members have been welcomed to the Board.

Mr Kenneth McDonald joined us in November of last year as Senior Executive and Miss Eileen Fraser was appointed in February as Financial Controller (Foreign Investment). Mr Johnston Forsyth will be retiring at the forthcoming Annual General Meeting. Mr Forsyth joined the Board in 1976 and was Vice Chairman from 1981 to 1987. He has made a significant contribution to the organisation over many years, for which we, the Board are extremely grateful. I take this opportunity of wishing him a healthy and happy retirement.

Our Management Staff have had a difficult year with the introduction of new management techniques. They have had to participate in many new aspects of organisational procedures and evaluation exercises over the last financial year. I am sure these new initiatives will be welcomed by staff at all levels in the very near future. On behalf of the Board I thank them for their continued effort and support.

FUTURE DEVELOPMENT PROGRAMME

Aldon Financial Services PLC, as a major financial force,

has the responsibility towards its shareholders (all groups), staff, customers and indeed to the country's economy as a whole. It is therefore the aim and the duty of the Board to achieve and maintain a level of profits as well as balance the interests of all the categories mentioned previously. The company therefore undertakes to increase investment in the home financial market with the object of achieving this stated aim as well as stimulating the Financial Services sector of the economy. Our development programme shows that we, as a public limited company, are committed to a 5-year programme of investment - £200m per annum will be invested from pre-tax profits or reserves in order to create a sound foundation from which to expand our range of financial services to all our current and potential shareholders and customers. A group of experts will monitor the progress of the investment programme to ensure that the return to the shareholder will continue in terms of dividend growth. I remain optimistic that this development programme will benefit many, if not all, of our client group and keep Aldon Financial Services PLC at the forefront of the Financial Services sector of the economy.

On behalf of the Board, may I express my thanks to you, the shareholders, for your continued support to our firm which has enabled us to progress from strength to strength over the last year and maintain a positive approach to the forthcoming year with optimism. We will consolidate on our previous experience to form the sound foundations upon which Aldon can build in the years ahead.

SPONSORSHIP

As well as investment in the economy, I am pleased to announce our continued commitment to sponsorship deals and packages throughout the world of sport and leisure activities. Aldon has just signed a sponsorship deal as the major sponsor of a leading international tennis tournament to be held during the summer of next year. This will be the fourth year in succession that we have been involved with this tournament but it will be the first time that we will be the main sponsor of the event.

A further feature of our development programme is a recent addition of a package for the promotion and sponsorship of the "Sport for the Disabled Week" during the second week of March next year. This will be another "first" for Aldon and we are delighted to be involved in such an important national event for disabled sportsmen and sportswomen. We have signed a deal worth £75,000 for this event which will help to promote the event from the beginning of next year.

Although these are the 2 major sponsorship deals, we will continue to be involved in a number of other packages as well as entering into some new sponsorships to keep the name of Aldon Financial Services PLC in a high profile in the sport and leisure arena throughout the country for another year.

The Board can assure all shareholders that the return on investment of such sponsorship deals and packages has been extremely worthwhile and benefits the

ASSIGNMENT 75
Recall ASS71 and display the text in 5 columns. Space between columns 10 mm. Left, right, top and bottom margins to be 25 mm. Delete Header and page numbers. Type specifications - AvantGarde 12 point. Print one copy of the first 2 pages. Save as ASS75.

H O M E IMPROVEMENTS

Living Area

Great scope exists for the householder to improve the decor within the living areas of the home. Wall papering, painting, wood cladding, plastering and door replacement are all areas where the homeowner can make considerable savings both in time and money. Suppliers are only too willing to offer suggestions both in the method of construction and in the design of the living areas. This not only reassures the individual but also can save time and extra expense.

The quality of self-assembly furniture has given even wider scope for the individual and a wide range of furniture can be purchased and assembled using only the minimum of tools. In all self-assembly packs, the instructions are clear and concise.

Kitchen Area

Although many householders will engage professional help when installing a new kitchen, it is nevertheless possible to design and purchase units for the kitchen area from the DIY store. Considerable time and care should be taken, however, when measuring for wall units and when wall measurements do not correspond to the unit sizes. Here again, however, the DIY enthusiast can undertake such a project knowing that expert advice and hints are readily available from the supplier.

Improving the kitchen is probably the most value-adding improvement which can be made within the home. Considering the amount of time spent in this area, it will also be one of the first areas of the home to be upgraded. Built-in or freestanding appliances can be costly additions to the home and will have such appliances as the washing machine, tumble dryer, dishwasher, fridge or freezer and a microwave oven.

Bathroom Area

A replacement bathroom will be determined by not only your current needs, but also the likely future requirements for the area. Modern bathroom equipment is available from the DIY store in a wide choice of styles, shapes and colours. Planning the bathroom is critical since this can often be the smallest area in the home. Will the installation of both a bath and a separate shower?

Pedestal basins are available in various sizes and shapes and can be either wall mounted or can be fitted in a corner. The WC cistern can often be concealed behind the wall thus adding to the available space within the bathroom. Apart from these basic items, some consideration must be given to the lighting within the bathroom. If in doubt, call in the experts.

G a r d e n Improvements

Most people enjoy

sitting in the garden on a warm day during the summer.

The addition of a patio area can enhance any property and all the materials necessary for the completion of such a project are readily available at all of our stores throughout the country.

Some plan must be prepared before making any purchases and it is recommended that c a r e f u l measurements are made and carefully noted. Any such development will add to the value of any property and will be an attractive feature in the garden.

Paving slabs are available in a wide range of size, colour, shape and surface.

You can choose from a wide range of natural colours - buff, grey, brown, yellow or slate. Many DIY enthusiasts will select a mixture of colours to give an appealing effect.

Sales of paving bricks have increased dramatically in recent months and many DIY persons are choosing these as an alternative to concrete slabs. They are small, easy to handle and can be arranged in a variety of patterns. Helpful information is always available from our building staff.

Double Glazing

A full range of quality double glazing for both windows and doors is now available from stock within our stores. There are many optional features and each pack comes with clear instructions for assembly. Heating costs have influenced many householders to invest in double glazing but quotations from double glazing firms may influence the DIY enthusiasts to tackle the project themselves.

There is a choice of wood, plastic or aluminium frames available and units will be prepared by our skilled glaziers.

Magnetic window framing is an alternative to the sealed units. The panel is easily fixed to the existing window frame and consequently saves considerable time and expense. The glazed panel can be easily removed for cleaning and can be opened to allow better air circulation within the room.

Perhaps the cheapest system is plastic film which comes in a variety of grades from a heavy duty plastic film to a fairly thin film. The latter should be used for small areas. The film is attached to the frame of the window and must be applied in warm weather so as to avoid any moisture being lodged between the film and the frame.

The choice is yours - you can spend as much or as little as you choose but make sure you select a style to match your existing windows as far as possible.

Central Heating

At all of our stores we have a large selection of radiators, boilers, thermostats etc - everything you might need to allow you to complete an installation. Planning of the heating system is obviously vital and we are able to supply you with details of recommended to install but are

ASSIGNMENT 76
Recall ASS72 and display the text in 5 columns. Space between columns 10 mm. Left, right, top and bottom margins to be 25 mm. Delete Header, Heading and page numbers. Type specifications - Palatino 12 point. Print one copy of both pages. Save as ASS76.

General Information

With the increasing amount of leisure time that is given to the general business community, it is important that this additional time is spent in a wise, healthy and enjoyable way. There's no better way to utilise this time than to participate in the art of "The Royal and Ancient Game". Lymac Golf and Leisure Promotion can offer a wide variety of options that will cater for all ages, male or female in the world of golf. Our aim is to provide our clients with the opportunity to play quality golf courses, obtain professional tuition, have fun and pleasure - all at affordable prices. We will also provide "off-the-course" entertainment for all of our clients, their families and guests while under contract with Lymac.

Courses

Lymac Golf and Leisure Promotion have acquired the reputation of being able to promote one of the largest selections of golf course availability to their clients. Over the last 15 years we have been able to achieve an unbeatable success rate in obtaining access to some of the most famous golfing links in a number of countries. Lymac concentrates its promotional activities at "the home of golf" - Scotland, but can also facilitate requests for other courses in the United Kingdom and indeed the remainder of the full international golfing arena, but plans are well ahead to enter into the United States of America in the next 2 years.

Leave the arrangements to us - we have the drive to book the course of your choice.

Equipment

Don't let the lack of equipment or difficulty of travel stand in your way - Lymac offer a full range of equipment-hire from a basic half-set of irons to tournament-grade clubs, bags, balls, trolleys and even electric "buggies" in your package. All the major suppliers of golf equipment are on hand to supply the equipment of your choice on request. As well as providing the hire of equipment, we will also supply each golfer with a Lymac Presentation Pack (free of charge). Each pack contains 6 golf balls, a golf glove, tees, markers and a club tie - all items have the Lymac logo. Should you require any additional items which have not been listed please contact our representative who will be happy to make the necessary arrangements to meet your requirements. We aim to please every golfer who registers with our firm and aim to make the choice of outing a time to remember.

Professionals - contact Lymac.

Competitions

During your stay with Lymac, various voluntary competitions will be available for the full range of golfer from the complete beginner to the low or scratch golfer. A small entry fee will be charged to each competitor in order that prizes can be awarded at the end of each competition. All of these competitions are designed for fun and will follow different formats including for example, medal play, 2-ball foursomes, mixed foursomes, stableford and match-play events.

For the keen golfer, The Lymac Open Tournament is played over the course of your choice (provided that it meets the specifications laid down by Lymac) on the first Saturday in August each year. This 18-hole medal competition is open to all golfers male and female (from scratch to 18 handicap) and offers substantial cash prizes to the eventual winners of each handicap section.

For further details of all the above competitions contact Lina Donald our Sales Executive on 0334 21462 or 0334 21767/8/9.

Other Leisure Provisions

As well as catering for the golfer, Lymac have pleasure in offering alternative leisure pursuits for the "non-golfer" at all the locations advertised in our annual brochure.

Each hotel used by our firm has leisure club facilities including heated indoor swimming pool, whirlpool spa, sauna, sunbeds, steam room and a wide variety of exercise equipment for all ages. The full range of activities is offered free of charge to all our clients.

However, if you are not of a sporting nature, Lymac will arrange other acitivities including excursions to various places of interest during the day as well as cinema and theatre outings in the evening. (An extra charge per head will be made for these additional activities.) Lymac also will keep your children amused during your stay as we have trained staff who will look after all children between 3 and 12 years of age. Activities during the day for children include swimming, mini golf, football, tennis, adventure playgrounds as well as a range of indoor games (all supervised by Lymac staff).

In the evening we will provide games and discos for the same age group as during the day. A babysitting/listening service is also available on request.

Lymac Golf and Leisure Promotion know how to make you and your party feel welcome and wish you a most enjoyable and relaxing holiday. Go home refreshed and ready to book your next outing with Lymac.

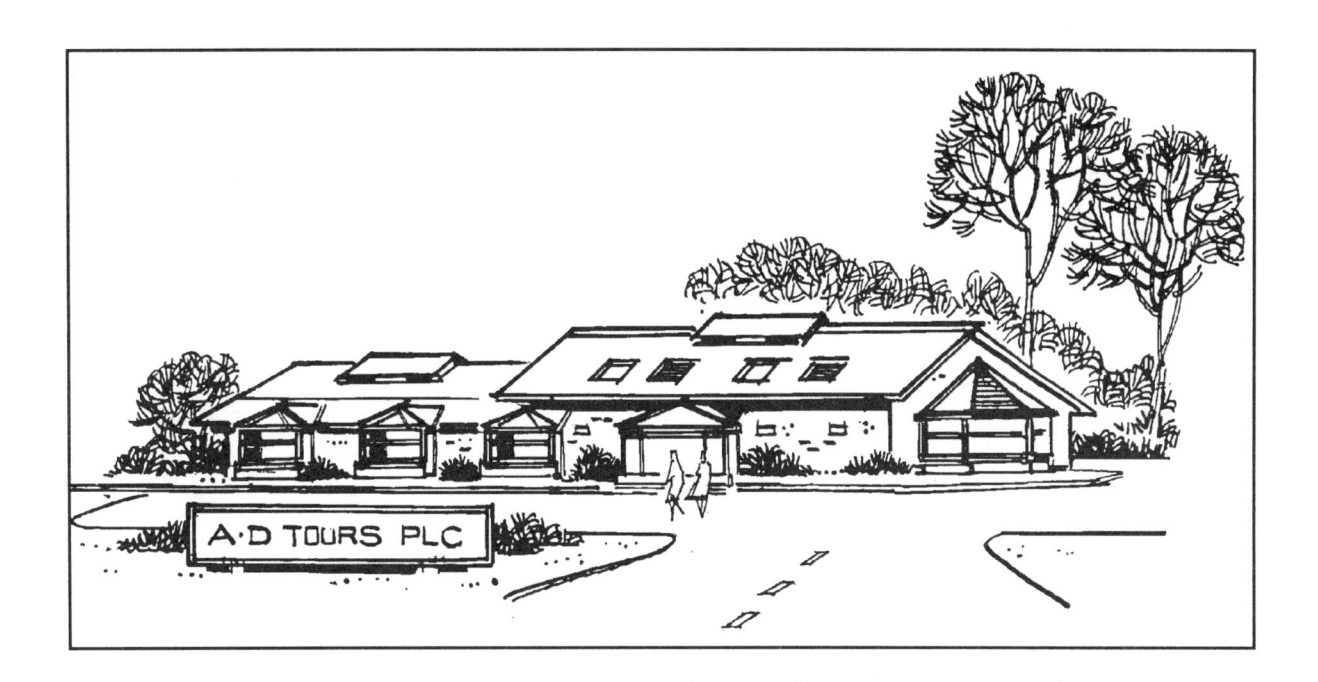

CHAIRMAN'S STATEMENT

INTRODUCTION

> ASSIGNMENT 77
> Recall Assignment 29.
> Scan the illustration (number 1) and fit to box.
> Print one copy. Save as ASS29.

Last year has seen a remarkable growth in our business to the extent that we have increased our sales force by 5 per cent to cope with the increased demand for our product. In recent years the demand for vacations has increased - customers are now taking short breaks as well as the traditional summer vacations. Our Management Team has improved the service to the customers by offering a wide and varied selection of reasonably priced holidays and the customer has responded by demanding better accommodation, better meals and improved travel arrangements. All of these have been taken on board by the Management Team and this has resulted in an increase in sales in what must be considered to be "an expanding market".

RESULTS

I am pleased to report to our stockholders that earnings per share have increased by 28 per cent. This has enabled us to declare a final dividend of 3.55 pence, giving an overall increase for the year of 10.5 per cent. This increase is the highest for a number of years and it indicates the confidence which exists within our Company. We are determined to increase the efficiency of our activities within the Company over the next 3 years. Our Management Team is strong with many new proposals coming forward for a maintenance of our market position. We aim to target Short Breaks next year with the emphasis being on an improved option choice within Scotland. We also aim to improve the selection of European locations for both short and long stay holidays.

I am confident that we can exploit the growth opportunities which these offer.

BOARD

Two new Directors have been appointed recently. Mrs Hilary Whyte has extensive knowledge of European holidays and Mr John Black brings extensive experience and knowledge of the home market.

Mrs Marion Duncan and Mr James Clive retired from the Board and we wish them well in their retirement.

CHAIRMAN'S STATEMENT

ASSIGNMENT 78
Recall ASS30.
Scan the illustration (number 2) and fit to box.
Print one copy. Save as ASS30.

INTRODUCTION

I am pleased to announce pre-tax profits for the year of £696 million. This is an increase of 6% on last year's figures. The post-tax figures for the current year have also shown a slight increase (1.5%) to £294 million which has covered the proposed dividend allowance for shareholders. As you will no doubt be aware the current market conditions, although slow, have improved and the prospects for next year appear to be brighter than first anticipated for our financial institution. Indeed, I would suggest that our organisation is in a much stronger position than many of our foreign competitors. This must be encouraging news for our shareholders and our customers alike.

Customers remain to be our top priority and this is reflected in the proposals and recommendations for the future as laid out in the Annual Report and Accounts.

BOARD

Since last year's report the Board have seen a number of changes. Two new members have been welcomed to the Board. Mr Kenneth McDonald joined us in November of last year as Senior Executive and Miss Eileen Fraser was appointed in February as Financial Controller (Foreign Investment). Mr Johnston Forsyth will be retiring at the forthcoming Annual General Meeting. Mr Forsyth joined the Board in 1976 and was Vice Chairman from 1981 to 1987. He has made a significant contribution to the organisation over many years, for which we, the Board are extremely grateful. I take this opportunity of wishing him a healthy and happy retirement.

STAFF

Our Management Staff have had a difficult year with the introduction of new management techniques. They have had to participate in many new aspects of organisational procedures and evaluation exercises over the last financial year. I am sure these new initiatives will be welcomed by staff at all levels in the very near future. On behalf of the Board I thank them for their continued effort and support.

HOME IMPROVEMENTS

Living Area

```
ASSIGNMENT 79
Recall ASS31.
Scan the illustration (number 3) and fit to box.
Print one copy. Save as ASS31.
```

Great scope exists for the householder to improve the decor within the living areas of the home. Wall papering, painting, wood cladding, plastering and door replacement are all areas where the homeowner can make considerable savings both in time and money. Suppliers are only too willing to offer suggestions both in the method of construction and in the design of the living areas. This not only reassures the individual but also can save time and extra expense.

The quality of self-assembly furniture has given even wider scope for the individual and a wide range of furniture can be purchased and assembled using only the minimum of tools. In all self-assembly packs, the instructions are clear and concise.

Kitchen Area

Although many householders will engage professional help when installing a new kitchen, it is nevertheless possible to design and purchase units for the kitchen area from the DIY store. Considerable time and care should be taken, however, when measuring for wall units and cupboards. Problems can arise when wall measurements do not correspond to the unit sizes. Here again, however, the DIY enthusiast can undertake such a project knowing that expert advice and hints are readily available from the supplier.

Improving the kitchen is probably the most value-adding improvement which can be made within the home. Considering the amount of time spent in this area, it will also be one of the first areas of the home to be upgraded. Built-in or freestanding appliances can be costly additions to the kitchen but the majority of homes will have such appliances as the washing machine, tumble dryer, dishwasher, fridge or freezer and a microwave oven.

Bathroom Area

A replacement bathroom will be determined by not only your current needs, but also the likely future requirements for the area. Modern bathroom equipment is available from the DIY store in a wide choice of styles, shapes and colours. Planning the bathroom is critical since this can often be the smallest area in the home. Will the size and shape of the room allow for the installation of both a bath and a separate shower?

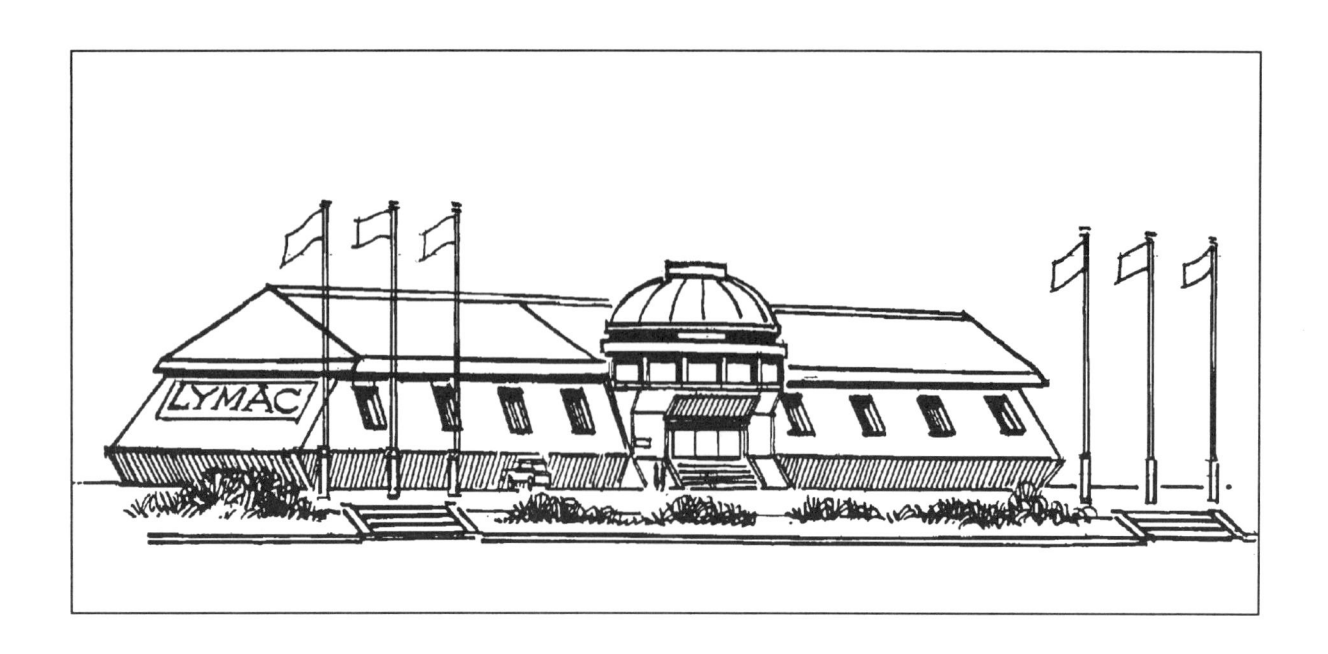

GOLF - "THE LYMAC WAY"

```
ASSIGNMENT 80
Recall ASS32.
Scan the illustration (number 4) and fit to box.
Print one copy.  Save as ASS32.
```

General Information

With the increasing amount of leisure time that is given to the general business community, it is important that this additional time is spent in a wise, healthy and enjoyable way. There's no better way to utilise this time than to participate in the art of "The Royal and Ancient Game". Lymac Golf and Leisure Promotion can offer a wide variety of options that will cater for all ages, male or female in the world of golf. Our aim is to provide our clients with the opportunity to play quality golf courses, obtain professional tuition, have fun and pleasure - all at affordable prices. We will also provide "off-the-course" entertainment for all of our clients, their families and guests while under contract with Lymac.

Courses

Lymac Golf and Leisure Promotion have acquired the reputation of being able to promote one of the largest selections of golf course availability to their clients. Over the last 15 years we have been able to achieve an unbeatable success rate in obtaining access to some of the most famous golfing links in a number of countries. Lymac concentrates its promotional activities at "the home of golf" - Scotland, but can also facilitate requests for other courses in the United Kingdom and indeed the remainder of Europe. As yet, we have not moved into the full international golfing arena, but plans are well ahead to enter into the United States of America in the next 2 years.

Leave the arrangements to us - we have the drive to book the course of your choice.

Equipment

Don't let the lack of equipment or difficulty of travel stand in your way - Lymac offer a full range of equipment-hire from a basic half-set of irons to tournament-grade clubs, bags, balls, trolleys and even electric "buggies" in your package. All the major suppliers of golf equipment are on contract with Lymac and we will guarantee to supply the equipment of your choice on request. We aim to please every golfer who registers with our firm and aim to make the choice of outing a time to remember.

If you want to be on par with the professionals - contact Lymac.

A & D TOURS PLC - Chairman's Statement

> ASSIGNMENT 81
> Recall ASS57.
> Scan the illustration (number 5) and position between column 1 and column 2 as shown.
> Custom wrap text as indicated.
> Print one copy of page 1. Save as ASS81.

CHAIRMAN'S STATEMENT

INTRODUCTION

Last year has seen a remarkable growth in our business to the extent that we have increased our sales force by 5 per cent to cope with the increased demand for our product. In recent years the demand for vacations has increased - customers are now taking short breaks as well as the traditional summer vacations. Our Management Team has improved the service to the customers by offering a wide and varied selection of reasonably priced holidays and the customer has responded by demanding better accommodation, better meals and improved travel arrangements. All of these have been taken on board by the Management Team and this has resulted in an increase in sales in what must be considered to be "an expanding market".

RESULTS

I am pleased to report to our stockholders that earnings per share have increased by 28 per cent. This has enabled us to declare a final dividend of 3.55 pence, giving an overall increase for the year of 10.5 per cent. This increase is the highest for a number of years and it indicates the confidence which exists within our Company. We are determined to increase the efficiency of our activities within the Company over the next 3 years.

Our Management Team is strong with many new proposals coming forward for a maintenance of our market position. We aim to target Short Breaks next year with the emphasis being on an improved option choice within Scotland. We also aim to improve the selection of European locations for both short and long stay holidays.

1

ALDON FINANCIAL SERVICES PLC - Chairman

> ASSIGNMENT 82
> Recall ASS58.
> Scan the illustration (number 6) and position between column 1 and column 2 as shown.
> Custom wrap text as indicated.
> Print one copy of page 1. Save as ASS82.

CHAIRMAN'S STATEMENT

INTRODUCTION

I am pleased to announce pre-tax profits for the year of £696 million. This is an increase of 6% on last year's figures. The post-tax figures for the current year have also shown a slight increase (1.5%) to £294 million which has covered the proposed dividend allowance for shareholders. As you will no doubt be aware the current market conditions, although slow, have improved and the prospects for next year appear to be brighter than first anticipated for our financial institution. Indeed, I would suggest that our organisation is in a much stronger position than many of our foreign competitors. This must be encouraging news for our shareholders and our customers alike.

Customers remain to be our top priority and this is reflected in the proposals and recommendations for the future as laid out in the Annual Report and Accounts.

Despite the previous financial year being difficult for most financial institutions, Aldon Financial Services PLC retained its share price and ended the year 9% above the FT All-Share Index (the third consecutive year that Aldon's Share Price has been above this index). Once again there was no call on shareholders (for the eighteenth consecutive year) and the dividend was increased by 11% on last year's figures. This development of progressive increases keeps our organisation in line with the objective stated in the Board's

DDA STORES PLC - The Impact of DC

> ASSIGNMENT 83
> Recall ASS 59.
> Scan the illustration (number 7) and position between column 1 and column 2 as shown.
> Custom wrap text as indicated.
> Print one copy of page 1. Save as ASS83.

HOME IMPROVEMENTS

Living Area

Great scope exists for the householder to improve the decor within the living areas of the home. Wall papering, painting, wood cladding, plastering and door replacement are all areas where the homeowner can make considerable savings both in time and money. Suppliers are only too willing to offer suggestions both in the method of construction and in the design of the living areas. This not only reassures the individual but also can save time and extra expense.

The quality of self-assembly furniture has given even wider scope for the individual and a wide range of furniture can be purchased and assembled using only the minimum of tools. In all self-assembly packs, the instructions are clear and concise.

Kitchen Area

Although many householders will engage professional help when installing a new kitchen, it is nevertheless possible to design and purchase units for the kitchen area from the DIY store. Considerable time and care should be taken, however, when measuring for wall units and cupboards. Problems can arise when wall measurements do not correspond to the unit sizes. Here again, however, the DIY enthusiast can undertake such a project knowing that expert advice and hints are readily available from the supplier.

Improving the kitchen is probably the most value-adding improvement which can be made within the home. Considering the amount of time spent in this area, it will also be one of the first areas of the home to be upgraded.

1

LYMAC Golf and Leisure Promotion

> ASSIGNMENT 84
> Recall ASS60.
> Scan the illustration (number 8) and position between column 1 and column 2 as shown.
> Custom wrap text as indicated.
> Print one copy of page 1. Save as ASS84.

GOLF - "THE LYMAC WAY"

General Information

With the increasing amount of leisure time that is given to the general business community, it is important that this additional time is spent in a wise, healthy and enjoyable way. There's no better way to utilise this time than to participate in the art of "The Royal and Ancient Game". Lymac Golf and Leisure Promotion can offer a wide variety of options that will cater for all ages, male or female in the world of golf. Our aim is to provide our clients with the opportunity to play quality golf courses, obtain professional tuition, have fun and pleasure - all at affordable prices. We will also provide "off-the-course" entertainment for all of our clients, their families and guests while under contract with Lymac.

Courses

Lymac Golf and Leisure Promotion have acquired the reputation of being able to promote one of the largest selections of golf course availability to their clients. Over the last 15 years we have been able to achieve an unbeatable success rate in obtaining access to some of the most famous golfing links in a number of countries.

A & D TOURS PLC

264 High Street
PERTH
PH12 3AG

ASSIGNMENT 85
Prepare the FORM OF PROXY on A4 landscape (2 copies).
Type specifications - Helvetica 10 point.
Print one copy. Save as ASS85.

FORM OF PROXY

Please read the accompanying leaflet before completing this form.

I/We hereby appoint the Chairman of the meeting or

_____

as my/our proxy to attend and vote for me/us at the annual general meeting of A & D Tours PLC to be held on and at any adjournment of the meeting.

Please indicate how your proxy should vote.

	For	Against
Resolution 1 To receive the directors' report and accounts	☐	☐
Resolution 2 To declare a final dividend	☐	☐
Resolution 3 To elect Mrs Irene Brown	☐	☐
Resolution 4 To re-elect Dr Robert Fleming	☐	☐
Resolution 5 To re-elect Mrs Pauline Hogarth	☐	☐
Resolution 6 To re-appoint the auditors and authorise the directors to fix the remuneration of the auditors	☐	☐

Signature .... Date ....

> ASSIGNMENT 86
> Prepare the COMPLIMENTS slip on A4 portrait (3 copies).
> Each slip to fit within a space of 180 x 80 mm.
> Type specifications - Times Roman 12 point.
> Print one copy. Save as ASS86.

DDA STORES PLC

150 Main Street
GLASGOW
G29 6TL

WITH COMPLIMENTS

Telephone 041-669 39528   Fax 041-625 42010

DDA STORES PLC

150 Main Street
GLASGOW
G29 6TL

WITH COMPLIMENTS

Telephone 041-669 39528   Fax 041-625 42010

DDA STORES PLC

150 Main Street
GLASGOW
G29 6TL

WITH COMPLIMENTS

Telephone 041-669 39528   Fax 041-625 42010

ASSIGNMENT 87

Prepare the ATTENDANCE CARD on A4 landscape (4 copies).
Each card to fit within a space of 130 mm x 95 mm.
Type specifications - Times Roman 10 point.
Print one copy. Save as ASS87.

ALDON FINANCIAL SERVICES PLC   **ATTENDANCE CARD**

Name ....

Address ....

If you intend to be in attendance at the Annual General Meeting at the New Theatre, High Street, Dundee on the last Friday of June, please complete this card by marking the appropriate boxes below, then send the card by return of post to Unit 8, New Industrial Estate, Dundee, DD5 7XJ.

If 2 or more persons intend to be in attendance, (any or all joint holders may attend) please enter the number in the space provided.

Signature .... | | I will attend

Date ....   Number attending

ALDON FINANCIAL SERVICES PLC   **ATTENDANCE CARD**

Name ....

Address ....

If you intend to be in attendance at the Annual General Meeting at the New Theatre, High Street, Dundee on the last Friday of June, please complete this card by marking the appropriate boxes below, then send the card by return of post to Unit 8, New Industrial Estate, Dundee, DD5 7XJ.

If 2 or more persons intend to be in attendance, (any or all joint holders may attend) please enter the number in the space provided.

Signature .... | | I will attend

Date ....   Number attending

ALDON FINANCIAL SERVICES PLC   **ATTENDANCE CARD**

Name ....

Address ....

If you intend to be in attendance at the Annual General Meeting at the New Theatre, High Street, Dundee on the last Friday of June, please complete this card by marking the appropriate boxes below, then send the card by return of post to Unit 8, New Industrial Estate, Dundee, DD5 7XJ.

If 2 or more persons intend to be in attendance, (any or all joint holders may attend) please enter the number in the space provided.

Signature .... | | I will attend

Date ....   Number attending

ALDON FINANCIAL SERVICES PLC   **ATTENDANCE CARD**

Name ....

Address ....

If you intend to be in attendance at the Annual General Meeting at the New Theatre, High Street, Dundee on the last Friday of June, please complete this card by marking the appropriate boxes below, then send the card by return of post to Unit 8, New Industrial Estate, Dundee, DD5 7XJ.

If 2 or more persons intend to be in attendance, (any or all joint holders may attend) please enter the number in the space provided.

Signature .... | | I will attend

Date ....   Number attending

ASSIGNMENT 88
Prepare the DISCOUNT VOUCHER on A4 portrait (8 copies).
Each voucher (including frame) to fit within a space of 80 mm x 60 mm.
Frame as shown with rounded corners.
Type specifications - AvantGarde 10 point.
Print one copy. Save as ASS88.

DDA STORES PLC

DISCOUNT VOUCHER

This entitles the holder

....

to a discount of 15%

on all purchases at any of our Stores

> **ASSIGNMENT 89**
> Prepare the PLAYING TICKET on A4 portrait (12 copies).
> Each ticket to fit within a space of 58 mm x 60 mm.
> Type specifications - Helvetica 9 point.
> Print one copy. Save as ASS89.

LYMAC Golf and Leisure Promotion

PLAYING TICKET

Golf Course ....

Date ....

GREEN FEE | £   : |

Representative's Signature

....

> **ASSIGNMENT 90**
> Prepare the REQUEST FORM on A4 portrait (2 copies).
> Type specifications - Times Roman 12 point.
> Print one copy. Save as ASS90.

REQUEST FOR COPY OF:
ANNUAL REPORT AND ACCOUNTS OF DIRECTORS

ALDON FINANCIAL SERVICES PLC
UNIT 8
New Industrial Estate
DUNDEE
DD5 7XJ

Shareholders who did not opt to receive the Annual Report and Accounts of Directors, but would now like a copy, can obtain one (or more) by completing the coupon below.

COMPLETE IN BLOCK CAPITALS. Return to ALDON FINANCIAL SERVICES PLC at the above address.

I wish to receive a copy of this year's Annual Report and Accounts of Directors ☐ YES ☐ NO

I wish to receive future copies of the Annual Report and Accounts of Directors ☐ YES ☐ NO

NAME .... ADDRESS ....

....

SHARE CERTIFICATE NUMBER(S) ....

Signature .... Date ....

REQUEST FOR COPY OF:
ANNUAL REPORT AND ACCOUNTS OF DIRECTORS

ALDON FINANCIAL SERVICES PLC
UNIT 8
New Industrial Estate
DUNDEE
DD5 7XJ

Shareholders who did not opt to receive the Annual Report and Accounts of Directors, but would now like a copy, can obtain one (or more) by completing the coupon below.

COMPLETE IN BLOCK CAPITALS. Return to ALDON FINANCIAL SERVICES PLC at the above address.

I wish to receive a copy of this year's Annual Report and Accounts of Directors ☐ YES ☐ NO

I wish to receive future copies of the Annual Report and Accounts of Directors ☐ YES ☐ NO

NAME .... ADDRESS ....

....

SHARE CERTIFICATE NUMBER(S) ....

Signature .... Date ....

ASSIGNMENT 91
Prepare the Receipt on A4 portrait
(3 copies).
Each slip to fit within a space of 180 x 75 mm.
Type specifications - Times Roman 10 point.
Print one copy. Save as ASS91.

LYMAC Golf and Leisure Promotion
Links Avenue
ST ANDREWS
Fife KY16 2CW

RECEIPT OF PAYMENT

Received with thanks the sum of £......... (Cash/Cheque/PO/Credit Card*) from ....
in payment of Accommodation/Equipment Hire/Green Fees/Tournament Fees/Other*

Signature .... (Cashier) Date .... * Delete as appropriate

---

LYMAC Golf and Leisure Promotion
Links Avenue
ST ANDREWS
Fife KY16 2CW

RECEIPT OF PAYMENT

Received with thanks the sum of £......... (Cash/Cheque/PO/Credit Card*) from ....
in payment of Accommodation/Equipment Hire/Green Fees/Tournament Fees/Other*

Signature .... (Cashier) Date .... * Delete as appropriate

---

LYMAC Golf and Leisure Promotion
Links Avenue
ST ANDREWS
Fife KY16 2CW

RECEIPT OF PAYMENT

Received with thanks the sum of £......... (Cash/Cheque/PO/Credit Card*) from ....
in payment of Accommodation/Equipment Hire/Green Fees/Tournament Fees/Other*

Signature .... (Cashier) Date .... * Delete as appropriate

ASSIGNMENT 92
Prepare the INTENT CARD on A4 landscape
(4 copies).
Each card to fit within a space of 120 mm x 75 mm.
Type specifications - Helvetica 8 point.
Print one copy. Save as ASS92.

DDA STORES PLC   **FORM OF INTENT**

I intend/do not intend being present at the annual general meeting on (*first Friday of August*).

Please delete as applicable, sign this form and return as soon as possible.

Final arrangements for the meeting will be sent out in due course.

Name ....

Address ....

Postcode .... Telephone Number ....

Signature ....

DDA STORES PLC   **FORM OF INTENT**

I intend/do not intend being present at the annual general meeting on (*first Friday of August*).

Please delete as applicable, sign this form and return as soon as possible.

Final arrangements for the meeting will be sent out in due course.

Name ....

Address ....

Postcode .... Telephone Number ....

Signature ....

DDA STORES PLC   **FORM OF INTENT**

I intend/do not intend being present at the annual general meeting on (*first Friday of August*).

Please delete as applicable, sign this form and return as soon as possible.

Final arrangements for the meeting will be sent out in due course.

Name ....

Address ....

Postcode .... Telephone Number ....

Signature ....

DDA STORES PLC   **FORM OF INTENT**

I intend/do not intend being present at the annual general meeting on (*first Friday of August*).

Please delete as applicable, sign this form and return as soon as possible.

Final arrangements for the meeting will be sent out in due course.

Name ....

Address ....

Postcode .... Telephone Number ....

Signature ....

ASSIGNMENT 93
Prepare the BUSINESS CARDS on A4 portrait (8 copies).
Each card (including frame) to fit within a space of 80 mm x 60 mm.
Frame as shown.
Type specifications - AvantGarde 10 point.
Print one copy. Save as ASS93.

A & D TOURS PLC

264 High Street
PERTH
PH12 3AG

Alison Wilkie
Travel Consultant

0738 692258 **0382 8856245**
Business **Home**

George Hamilton
Travel Consultant

0738 692258 **0738 8866321**
Business **Home**

A & D TOURS PLC

264 High Street
PERTH
PH12 3AG

Alison Wilkie
Travel Consultant

0738 692258 **0382 8856245**
Business **Home**

A & D TOURS PLC

264 High Street
PERTH
PH12 3AG

George Hamilton
Travel Consultant

0738 692258 **0738 8866321**
Business **Home**

A & D TOURS PLC

264 High Street
PERTH
PH12 3AG

Alison Wilkie
Travel Consultant

0738 692258 **0382 8856245**
Business **Home**

A & D TOURS PLC

264 High Street
PERTH
PH12 3AG

George Hamilton
Travel Consultant

0738 692258 **0738 8866321**
Business **Home**

A & D TOURS PLC

264 High Street
PERTH
PH12 3AG

Alison Wilkie
Travel Consultant

0738 692258 **0382 8856245**
Business **Home**

A & D TOURS PLC

264 High Street
PERTH
PH12 3AG

George Hamilton
Travel Consultant

0738 692258 **0738 8866321**
Business **Home**

> ASSIGNMENT 94
> Prepare the BUSINESS CARDS on A4 portrait (10 copies).
> Each card (including frame) to fit within a space of 85 mm x 40 mm.
> Type specifications - Palatino 6 point. Names in Palatino 12 point. (Italic and bold).
> Print one copy. Save as ASS94.

Allan Williams
Managing Director

LYMAC Golf and Leisure Promotion
Links Avenue
ST ANDREWS
Fife KY16 2CW

Telephone:
Direct Line 0334 21767-9
Mobile 0334 21377
Fax 0334 21990

Lina Donald
Sales Executive

LYMAC Golf and Leisure Promotion
Links Avenue
ST ANDREWS
Fife KY16 2CW

Telephone:
Direct Line 0334 21767-9
Mobile 0334 21462
Fax 0334 21990

Allan Williams
Managing Director

LYMAC Golf and Leisure Promotion
Links Avenue
ST ANDREWS
Fife KY16 2CW

Telephone:
Direct Line 0334 21767-9
Mobile 0334 21377
Fax 0334 21990

Lina Donald
Sales Executive

LYMAC Golf and Leisure Promotion
Links Avenue
ST ANDREWS
Fife KY16 2CW

Telephone:
Direct Line 0334 21767-9
Mobile 0334 21462
Fax 0334 21990

Allan Williams
Managing Director

LYMAC Golf and Leisure Promotion
Links Avenue
ST ANDREWS
Fife KY16 2CW

Telephone:
Direct Line 0334 21767-9
Mobile 0334 21377
Fax 0334 21990

Lina Donald
Sales Executive

LYMAC Golf and Leisure Promotion
Links Avenue
ST ANDREWS
Fife KY16 2CW

Telephone:
Direct Line 0334 21767-9
Mobile 0334 21462
Fax 0334 21990

Allan Williams
Managing Director

LYMAC Golf and Leisure Promotion
Links Avenue
ST ANDREWS
Fife KY16 2CW

Telephone:
Direct Line 0334 21767-9
Mobile 0334 21377
Fax 0334 21990

Lina Donald
Sales Executive

LYMAC Golf and Leisure Promotion
Links Avenue
ST ANDREWS
Fife KY16 2CW

Telephone:
Direct Line 0334 21767-9
Mobile 0334 21462
Fax 0334 21990

Allan Williams
Managing Director

LYMAC Golf and Leisure Promotion
Links Avenue
ST ANDREWS
Fife KY16 2CW

Telephone:
Direct Line 0334 21767-9
Mobile 0334 21377
Fax 0334 21990

Lina Donald
Sales Executive

LYMAC Golf and Leisure Promotion
Links Avenue
ST ANDREWS
Fife KY16 2CW

Telephone:
Direct Line 0334 21767-9
Mobile 0334 21462
Fax 0334 21990

A & D TOURS PLC

664 High Street
PERTH   PH12 3AG

Telephone (0738) 692258
Fax (0738) 613887

ASSIGNMENT 95
Prepare the BOOKING FORM on A4 portrait following layout as indicated.
Type specifications - Times Roman 10 point.
Print one copy. Save as ASS95.

BOOKING FORM

Please complete all sections in BLOCK CAPITALS

Name   ....

Address   ....

           ....

Section 1 - Party Details			
Mr/Mrs/Miss/Ms	Initials	Surname	Age
1			
2			
3			
4			
5			

Section 2 - Holiday Details				
	Reference	Resort	Date from	Date to
1st Choice				
2nd Choice				

Section 3 - Deposit and Confirmation Statement

Please reserve the accommodation for all persons above. I enclose a Cheque/Money Order/Credit Card details for £............ being deposit of £50 per person.

Signed .... Date ....

Section 4 - Payment Details - For Office Use Only

Reservation Reference	Total Cost	Insurance Charges	Deposit Paid	Balance due

ALDON FINANCIAL SERVICES PLC

UNIT 8
New Industrial Estate
DUNDEE
DD5 7XJ

Telephone (0382) 480435
Fax (0382) 253345

FLEXIBLE SAVINGS PLAN APPLICATION FORM

Please complete in BLOCK CAPITALS

SECTION A		
Mr/Mrs/Miss/Ms	Forename(s)	Surname
Address		
Telephone Number	Home	Work
Date of Birth		Sex
Occupation		

SECTION B

Please tick appropriate box

		YES	NO
1	Have you consulted your doctor within the last 3 years for other than minor ailments?	☐	☐
2	Are you currently taking medication or drugs?	☐	☐
3	Have you ever had life, accident or sickness insurance rejected by another firm?	☐	☐

(If the answer to any of the above is YES, please give full details overleaf)

INVESTMENT REQUIRED

Please indicate the monthly investment required (Tick Box)

£50 ☐   £40 ☐   £30 ☐   £20 ☐   Any other amount (please state) £ ☐

DECLARATION: I declare that, to the best of my knowledge and belief, the statements above are true.

Signature	Date

ASSIGNMENT 96
Prepare the APPLICATION FORM on A4 portrait following layout as indicated.
Type specifications - Bookman 10 point.
Print one copy. Save as ASS96.

DDA STORES PLC

150 Main Street
GLASGOW
G29 6TL

Telephone 041-669 39528
Fax 041-625 42010

> ASSIGNMENT 97
> Prepare the ORDER FORM on A4 portrait following layout as indicated.
> Type specifications - Times Roman 10 point.
> Print one copy. Save as ASS97.

ORDER FORM

Name ....

Address ....

.... Postcode ....

Telephone Number Day .... Evening ....

Page Number	Description	Ref Number	Quantity	Size	Price

FOR OFFICE USE ONLY					
Order Received		Price Checked	To Sales	Order Sent	Invoice Sent

LYMAC Golf and Leisure Promotion

Links Avenue
ST ANDREWS
Fife
KY16 2CW

ASSIGNMENT 98
Prepare the ENTRY FORM on A4 portrait following layout as indicated.
Type specifications - Bookman 10 point.
Print one copy. Save as ASS98.

ENTRY FORM

THE LYMAC OPEN TOURNAMENT

This is an 18-hole medal competition for both male and female golfers (maximum handicap allowance - 18 strokes). The competition can be played on any 18-hole golf course (more than 7,000 yards long with a minimum par 71) on the first Saturday in August. Entry fee is £15 per person.

SCRATCH AND HANDICAP PRIZES (Vouchers)

1st Prize £300   2nd Prize £200   3rd Prize £100   4th Prize £50

I wish to enter the person/s named below for the Lymac Open. I confirm that the course meets the above criteria and that the lowest handicap specified for each entrant listed is correct. I enclose a Cheque/Postal Order Number .... for £.............. made payable in favour of "Lymac GLP".

Name .... Signature

Position .... Date

NAME	HANDICAP (maximum 18)	FEE

FOR OFFICE USE

Number of Entries Received   Total Fees Paid   Initials

A & D TOURS PLC

664 High Street
PERTH   PH12 3AG

Telephone (0738) 692258
Fax (0738) 613887

ASSIGNMENT 99
Recall ASS95.
Scan the illustration (number 9) and position as indicated.
Print one copy. Save as ASS99.

BOOKING FORM

Please complete all sections in BLOCK CAPITALS

Name ....

Address ....

....

Section 1 - Party Details			
Mr/Mrs/Miss/Ms	Initials	Surname	Age
1			
2			
3			
4			
5			

Section 2 - Holiday Details				
	Reference	Resort	Date from	Date to
1st Choice				
2nd Choice				

Section 3 - Deposit and Confirmation Statement

Please reserve the accommodation for all persons above. I enclose a Cheque/Money Order/Credit Card details for £ .... being deposit of £50 per person.

Signed .... Date ....

Section 4 - Payment Details - For Office Use Only

Reservation Reference	Total Cost	Insurance Charges	Deposit Paid	Balance due

ALDON FINANCIAL SERVICES PLC

UNIT 8
New Industrial Estate
DUNDEE
DD5 7XJ

ASSIGNMENT 100
Recall ASS96.
Scan the illustration (number 10) and position as indicated.
Print one copy. Save as ASS100.

Telephone (0382) 480435
Fax (0382) 253345

FLEXIBLE SAVINGS PLAN APPLICATION FORM

Please complete in BLOCK CAPITALS

SECTION A		
Mr/Mrs/Miss/Ms	Forename(s)	Surname
Address		
Telephone Number	Home	Work
Date of Birth		Sex
Occupation		

SECTION B

Please tick appropriate box

                                                            YES   NO

1   Have you consulted your doctor within the last 3 years for other than minor ailments? ☐ ☐

2   Are you currently taking medication or drugs? ☐ ☐

3   Have you ever had life, accident or sickness insurance rejected by another firm? ☐ ☐

(If the answer to any of the above is YES, please give full details overleaf)

INVESTMENT REQUIRED

Please indicate the monthly investment required (Tick Box)

£50 ☐   £40 ☐   £30 ☐   £20 ☐   Any other amount (please state) £ ☐

DECLARATION: I declare that, to the best of my knowledge and belief, the statements above are true.

Signature	Date

DDA STORES PLC

150 Main Street
GLASGOW
G29 6TL

Telephone 041-669 39528
Fax 041-625 42010

> ASSIGNMENT 101
> Recall ASS97.
> Scan the illustration (number 11) and position as indicated.
> Print one copy. Save as ASS101.

ORDER FORM

Name ....

Address ....

.... Postcode ....

Telephone Number Day .... Evening ....

Page Number	Description	Ref Number	Quantity	Size	Price

FOR OFFICE USE ONLY

Order Received	Price Checked	To Sales	Order Sent	Invoice Sent

LYMAC Golf and Leisure Promotion

Links Avenue
ST ANDREWS
Fife
KY16 2CW

ASSIGNMENT 102
Recall ASS98.
Scan the illustration (number 12) and position as indicated.
Print one copy. Save as ASS102.

LGLP

ENTRY FORM

THE LYMAC OPEN TOURNAMENT

This is an 18-hole medal competition for both male and female golfers (maximum handicap allowance - 18 strokes). The competition can be played on <u>any</u> 18-hole golf course (more than 7,000 yards long with a minimum par 71) on the first Saturday in August. Entry fee is £15 per person.

SCRATCH AND HANDICAP PRIZES (Vouchers)

1st Prize £300   2nd Prize £200   3rd Prize £100   4th Prize £50

I wish to enter the person/s named below for the Lymac Open. I confirm that the course meets the above criteria and that the lowest handicap specified for each entrant listed is correct. I enclose a Cheque/Postal Order Number .... for £............. made payable in favour of "Lymac GLP".

Name .... Signature

Position .... Date

NAME	HANDICAP (maximum 18)	FEE

FOR OFFICE USE

Number of Entries Received   Total Fees Paid   Initials

ASSIGNMENT 103
Scan in illustration (Number 1). This will be required for Assignment 77.
Save as appropriate.

ASSIGNMENT 104
Scan in illustration (Number 2). This will be required for Assignment 78.
Save as appropriate.

ASSIGNMENT 105
Scan in illustration (Number 3). This will be required for Assignment 79. Save as appropriate.

ASSIGNMENT 106
Scan in illustration (Number 4). This will be required for Assignment 80. Save as appropriate.

ASSIGNMENT 108
Scan in illustration (Number 6). This will be required for Assignment 82. Save as appropriate.

ASSIGNMENT 107
Scan in illustration (Number 5). This will be required for Assignment 81. Save as appropriate.

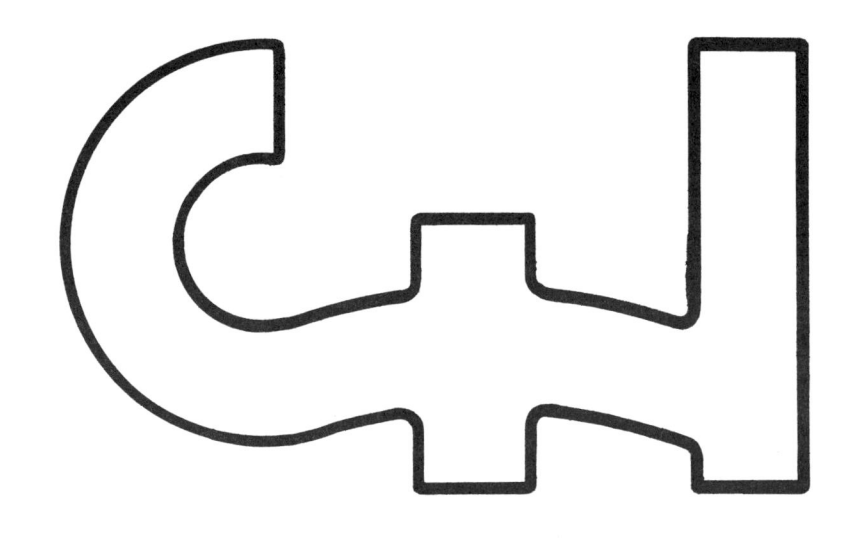

ASSIGNMENT 110
Scan in illustration (Number 8). This will be required for Assignment 84.
Save as appropriate.

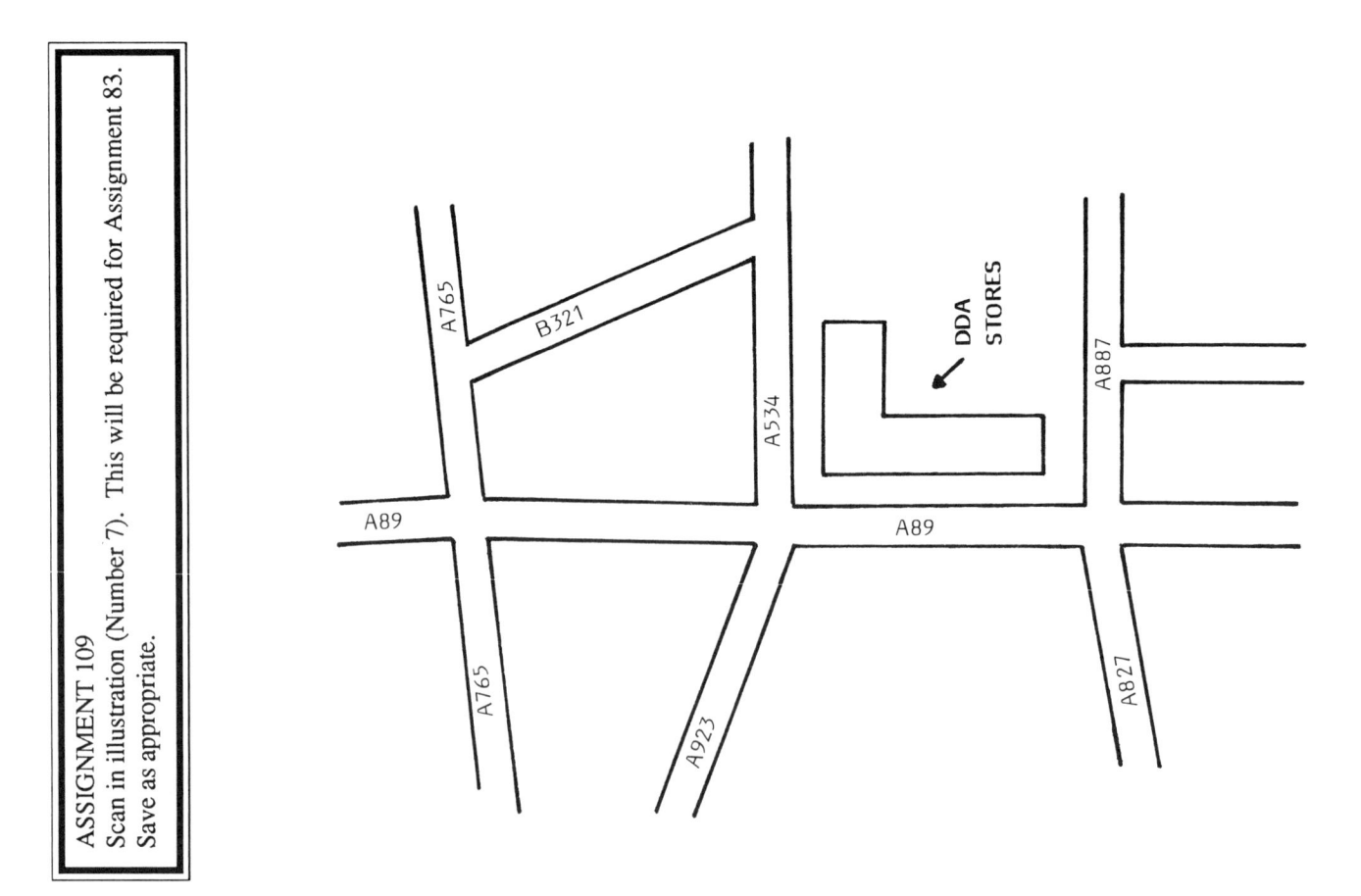

ASSIGNMENT 109
Scan in illustration (Number 7). This will be required for Assignment 83.
Save as appropriate.

ASSIGNMENT 111
Scan in illustration (Number 9). This will be required for Assignment 99.
Save as appropriate.

ASSIGNMENT 112
Scan in illustration (Number 10). This will be required for Assignment 100.
Save as appropriate.

ASSIGNMENT 113
Scan in illustration (Number 11). This will be required for Assignment 101.
Save as appropriate.

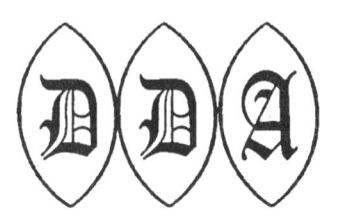

ASSIGNMENT 114
Scan in illustration (Number 12). This will be required for Assignment 102.
Save as appropriate.